Why Are People Afraid of Love?

Rev. Tony K. Thomas

Copyright © 2019 Rev. Tony K. Thomas.

All rights reserved. No part of this book may be used or reproduced by any means, graphic, electronic, or mechanical, including photocopying, recording, taping or by any information storage retrieval system without the written permission of the author except in the case of brief quotations embodied in critical articles and reviews.

This book is a work of non-fiction. Unless otherwise noted, the author and the publisher make no explicit guarantees as to the accuracy of the information contained in this book and in some cases, names of people and places have been altered to protect their privacy.

Unless otherwise indicated, all scripture quotations taken from the New American Standard Bible® (NASB), Copyright © 1960, 1962, 1963, 1968, 1971, 1972, 1973, 1975, 1977, 1995 by The Lockman Foundation Used by permission. www.Lockman.org

Scripture marked (KJV) taken from the King James Version of the Bible.

Scripture quotations marked (TLB) are taken from The Living Bible copyright © 1971. Used by permission of Tyndale House Publishers, Inc., Carol Stream, Illinois 60188. All rights reserved.

Scripture quotations marked (AMP) are taken from the Amplified Bible, Copyright © 1954, 1958, 1962, 1964, 1965, 1987 by The Lockman Foundation. Used by permission.

Scripture quotations marked (AMPCE) are taken from the Amplified Bible, Copyright © 1954, 1958, 1962, 1964, 1965, 1987 by The Lockman Foundation. Used by permission.

Scripture quotations marked (GNT) are from the Good News Translation in Today's English Version- Second Edition Copyright © 1992 by American Bible Society. Used by Permission.

Scripture quotations marked MSG are taken from THE MESSAGE, copyright © 1993, 1994, 1995, 1996, 2000, 2001, 2002 by Eugene H. Peterson. Used by permission of NavPress. All rights reserved. Represented by Tyndale House Publishers, Inc.

WestBow Press books may be ordered through booksellers or by contacting:

WestBow Press
A Division of Thomas Nelson & Zondervan
1663 Liberty Drive
Bloomington, IN 47403
www.westbowpress.com
1 (866) 928-1240

Because of the dynamic nature of the Internet, any web addresses or links contained in this book may have changed since publication and may no longer be valid. The views expressed in this work are solely those of the author and do not necessarily reflect the views of the publisher, and the publisher hereby disclaims any responsibility for them.

Any people depicted in stock imagery provided by Getty Images are models, and such images are being used for illustrative purposes only.
Certain stock imagery © Getty Images.

ISBN: 978-1-9736-4832-1 (sc)
ISBN: 978-1-9736-4833-8 (hc)
ISBN: 978-1-9736-4831-4 (e)

Library of Congress Control Number: 2018914569

Print information available on the last page.

WestBow Press rev. date: 1/2/2019

DEDICATION

I speak grace: grace to the mountains that have stood before me but now have been moved. I can't say enough about the goodness and mercy that come from our heavenly King. It is a great pleasure that I bow before Him and acknowledge that He is Lord of my life and guides me in my daily decisions. Jesus called me into Christian ministry on August 8, 1982. He commissioned that I should proclaim His glory to those who can't see it and proclaim happiness for those who only know grief, pain and misery, for all shall be made new through His mercies and riches in glory.

I can say that I have walked in this commission, and I am here to make known within this world the glory of our King. Never did I know that I would be entering a time when Christians can shout to the Lord and learn of His blessings, which are for us, and still remain in pain and misery deep within our souls. Nor did I realize there are many in this world that have obtained great successes and amassed great wealth but still are not happy or content within their souls.

Before I surrendered my life to Christ, I was involved in a life of recreational drugs use and misuse of time during my formative adolescent years. Therefore, I believed, after being called, that my commission was leading me to be a voice to those who are bounded or have been afflicted by drug and alcohol addictions. I found myself ministering in prisons and working as a volunteer with Christian rehab ministries. I knocked on doors. I walked the streets, proclaiming the good news of the gospel to whosoever would, using bullhorn, tracks, T-shirts, hats, and even radio and TV broadcasts to those whom I perceived as outcasts, outlaws, and miserable in life.

However, I was unaware that many of the downtrodden carried pains and fears from many failed relationships. This included those who attended church regularly and those who didn't go to church at all. It even included ministers of the gospel of Christ. I began to see a harvest of hearts that desired one thing: to discover Love in their lives.

This brings to my memory a popular passage from Psalm 34, which now means so much more:

> The LORD is near to the brokenhearted
> And saves those who are crushed in spirit.
> Many are the afflictions of the righteous,
> But the LORD delivers him out of them all. (Ps. 34:18–19)

As this world enters the most prosperous age ever known to mankind, the pain and misery of broken relationships are increasingly becoming a societal norm. So many have felt the effects of brokenness of hearts, lives, and families brought on by divorce and failed relationships. Society often keeps a record and gives a number to what is referred to as the divorce rate. However, there is no number to record the rate for failed relationships that never develop into lasting and harmonious Love. I believe that we are witnessing a global epidemic of failed relationships that will be detrimental to our society's well-being.

Therefore, I dedicate this book to those who have been crushed, heartbroken, and afflicted in their life's search for Love. I know that the Lord shall deliver each out of all their afflictions. I believe this book is just a tool, a step to begin the process of removing the lingering fear and torment that can keep each from discovering the greatest gift of all—Love.

I capitalize Love because I believe Love is a person and a place in each of our lives. Love is always present, but can't be seen from the looming clouds of despair. As you read this book, may the Spirit of God begin to open your mind, soul, and spirit to receive and be reassured of the Love of God. It's my intent to remind all that God is Love. No matter what you have faced or what you have been through, know this: agape Love will remove all your fears. Love still exists and is never going anyplace except into the hearts of those who will receive it and give it to another.

Therefore, I dedicate this book to you, the brokenhearted; to you who have known grief, pain, and misery from broken relationships.

Now, I know that the Lord's commission to me on August 8, 1982, is being fulfilled—not by my past, but by His calling. This is a heavenly work. It will reveal His mercy and riches, which are in glory for those who read this book and do the work of removing the fear of Love from their souls.

His glory has guided you to this step of faith. It is time to say goodbye to all the grief, pain, and misery that has been collected throughout your love life. The Bible states that nothing can separate us from the Love of God. So get ready to reset your mind and renew your spirit for new chapters of Love to be written in your life.

This book is for those who are sick and tired of starting and stopping and progressing no further in relationship building. Perhaps it is time to stop the self-diagnosis and ignoring the pain and fears that has lingered from past failed relationships. Jesus said that "it is not those who are healthy who need a physician, but those who are sick" (Matt. 9:12). Be reminded that Jesus can heal the brokenhearted. This book is not just for Christians, but for everyone who wants to stop the blame game and begin to eradicate the fears and struggles that have prohibited the development of a lasting Love. However, I believe that before you finish this work, you will recognize the need to allow and accept God's guidance in developing true Love. This will always begin with accepting Jesus Christ as Lord and Savior of your soul. For we all know that God so loved the world that He gave His only Son for the forgiveness of this world's sins. We all know that fears are real, so let's learn that Love is just as real.

You, deciding to read this book, show that you desire and have a renewed expectation of developing lasting Love. I believe this is your time to look inside and get some answers to those questions that you always thought about but seldom sought to find. Perhaps you picked this book up out of curiosity. I believe you will discover that the joys of developing a lasting Love in your life are just a prayer away.

A remnant of Love still lingering within our souls is enough to spark an eternal flame, once it is ignited by the right connections. That first connection needs to be with the Giver of Love, who prepares us to become more loving and lovable. I believe this book will be a source to help you reconnect with yourself and grow into that lovable person, by learning to manage and loosen the grip of fear each time it appears. Afterward, we should be able to attract and assist in someone else's hopes for the same. Once you get that beam of fear out of your eye, you will see clearly how to get that speck of fear out of another's eye.

You are about to be rewarded with the faith that can move mountains, which works by Love. Your prayers and faith have drawn you to this material, and it is now time to allow the seeds of Love to be sown within your good heart. Might your love life begin to blossom and produce thirty-, sixty-, and a hundredfold in return? Might the force of Love restore to you seven times what the force of fear has taken or kept you from receiving? This is your season of harvest, so get ready. The best is yet to come. For His mercy has guided you to discover the riches of His glory, so you may witness true happiness in your love life.

Remember this: His mercy endures forever! And Love never fails.
APPTE
Rev. Tony K. Thomas

CONTENTS

Introduction xiii

Chapter 1 A Sign of the Times 1
Chapter 2 What Love Is. 13
Chapter 3 Move Forth and Say No More 31
Chapter 4 Our Upbringing 45
Chapter 5 Definition of Love 61
Chapter 6 Love Has to Be Given. 85
Chapter 7 Love Is an Action, Not just a Feeling 99
Chapter 8 Now Is the Time. 115

Conclusion 125
Acknowledgments. 133
About Rev. Tony K. Thomas 137

THE FORCE OF LOVE

Love can't be seen
Love can't be measured
Love can't be bottled
Love can't be manufactured

Yet it exists in all
Without boundary or limit
It can't be lifted
By the muscles of men

It is controlled by its own laws
Throughout the universe it is known
It lives only in our hearts
Where there it belongs

It moves faster than the wind
Stronger than a volcano
Hotter than fire
Burning longer than a coal

Often it is blamed
When it was never involved
Many times misquoted
When it didn't speak at all

Its force is with us
When used by its laws
Given only from above
Making it the greatest gift of all—
Love

Priceless Production

INTRODUCTION

Thirty-six years ago, after I gave my life to Christ, the Spirit of God impressed upon me that I was not to seek to write books. After that, I never gave writing any consideration. I enjoyed studying and teaching the flock of God. I write my own messages by the unction of the Holy Spirit, and many are recorded for the ministry's weekly television and radio broadcast called *Heal Our Land*. That was it. I continued with the mindset of no publications. I have mentioned this to many people, including my daughters and church family. As a messenger of the kingdom of God, I never seek attention or notoriety or fame.

    I recently found out that God guided my soul, so I wouldn't minister to seek big business but simply God's business. God knows exactly what He is doing, even when we can't recognize it or see where He is leading us in this journey of life. He knew that during my time of salvation, I was about to enter the book writing craze of humankind.

    Today, books are written by just about everyone to validate their authority. I have found that on any issue one may face, there are authors who assume that others will benefit if they write a book. God knew this. He was protecting and preparing me to deliver a true message from His throne room at the appointed time, by allowing His Word to become my source in life through many seasons.

    Then in August 2005, during the aftermath of Hurricane Katrina, I went to Bible study and found that no one was there. I was upset that someone had called off the class at a time when the nation was in need of prayer. I walked around the church, at Foundation of Power Outreach Ministries in Sanford, North Carolina, perturbed and whining to God about no one being there. As I was about to leave, I felt a holy presence speak to me and say these words: "Son, I am here."

These are the moments when you feel small in the holy presence of the Anointed One. You can't take back your thoughts or your actions. It's like you are snapped back into the reality of who is really in control and is the reason that you are at church in the first place.

After falling on my face and acknowledging His presence, I began to crawl like a snail toward the front of the church. I got my mind past my initial concerns and heard Him impress upon me that it was now time to begin to prepare to write books for the kingdom of God. I heard from within my soul what the Spirit was saying to me. He knew that I would struggle with this assignment because of the previous direction given to me. However, I believed that the Spirit would use, speak to, and guide me in the writing of these books. I felt that I was being directed to prepare to write the books for the glory of the kingdom of heaven.

Then I was given a prophetic word concerning the flood's aftermath. It was revealed to my spirit from within my soul that "there is a storm coming, not for destruction but for salvation." Then the Spirit's anointing was lifted. I arose to gather my things, exit the church building, and start my drive home.

Afterward, I mentioned these words to the congregation. I asked them to tell me which subjects they'd heard me speak about that they thought other people would benefit from. I didn't hear back from anyone.

God knew that this would be a very difficult task for me. Literally, I have spoken and written thousands of messages by the guidance of the Holy Spirit during my ministry. However, at that moment, I couldn't even begin to think of what to say or write in a book.

Years passed. Then, in 2011, the Spirit of the Lord revealed to me that my initial topic would be Love and relationship building. I knew that I would have to rely on Him do this through me, because these are the very areas in which I am the least and the weakest. *I am no expert by any means.* I feel more like a fool or failure because of my past pains and unsuccessful relationships.

I became afraid to write or even begin to perform this task because of my own broken heart and afflictions. I put it off and merely prayed about it. Ironically, at the time of His direction, I was in a miserable and painful season in life. I was recovering from a broken relationship. He was just restoring my heart. I am reminded that God chooses the foolish and weak to confound the wise and strong. The Holy Spirit needs only a willing vessel to use for His works and purposes.

After much pressure had built up—or let's just say anxiety—over writing and putting my name out in the wide world, the Spirit of the Lord let me know that I had already written many books. He reminded me that in 2007, He instructed me to start typing, saving each message in a Microsoft Word document. I had placed in notebooks all of my messages for each year. Therefore, I had already written many books' worth of words.

I have learned to pray, ask, seek, and knock when I am given a task or an opportunity that is beyond my abilities. Recently, I was having a moment with completing the first book, *Loneliness: God's Gift to the Single*. It was like I couldn't let go of what God had put inside of me to share with the world. I decided to do a search on YouTube about publishing a book.

A minister of notoriety came up in my search. He is now deceased. I had never listened to his messages before, but that particular night it was like he was speaking directly to me from the realm of eternity. He said, "Most of you have already written books because you speak to people." He said that you must write, in reproducible media, everything that you speak or want to speak to an audience. He went on to describe the importance of books and how they will live forever. Then he mentioned that God wrote the most important book, using human souls inspired by the Holy Spirit to record His written Word.

When I heard this, I had to listen to it again several times. I sensed that the pressures of moving forward were being removed from my mind. Also, I realized that this was confirmation as to why the Holy Spirit had guided me years before into typing and saving my messages. As you can now understand, I am a bit slow when it comes to really listening to and obeying the instructions that the Lord gives to me.

Recently, the Spirit brought back to my remembrance that in 2005, He revealed to me that I should prepare to write and publish books. It dawned upon me that He didn't want me to publish any of my former messages, but to prepare for a totally new message. In 2005, I was just beginning my journey of singleness after being married for more than half my life. It never occurred to me until July 2018 that God was using my single journey to prepare me for the work to share with the world.

I can look back and see that He will guide a person into His true purposes; He revealed to me there would be books, not only one book. Today, I have written two books. I'm about the begin a third on the subject of Love.

God shared with me that the reason I was chosen was because He knew that I would pay attention to details. I have done so. I can recall most conversations with the many souls I have met along this journey of singleness. I could see the pitfalls in their choices, and I used what I saw as a guide to avoid the same pitfalls.

The years it has taken to write these books weren't my doing, but His. I needed them all to prepare me for the work and the writing. I believe that those who read and allow the Holy Spirit to speak to their souls will find in this book a new spiritual medicine to heal and reset their love lives.

This book is for the Lord's glory. It is His desire that the world learn of His true nature—that He is Love. There is a popular song that says, "What the world needs now is love, sweet love." While the world, even the Christians in the world, seek more Love, many souls are falling in the trap of being afraid to love. This book addresses this question that few ever ask: "Why are people afraid of Love?" or "Why am I afraid of Love?" This question is especially pertinent in this generation, in which there is a worldwide epidemic of failed relationships.

Perhaps this book will speak to you. Perhaps it will inspire you to look inside and make some needed personal adjustment when it comes to relationship building. I am no expert, but I am a servant and survivor. I am being obedient and looking forward to learning more to remove all the fears that have kept me from loving with all my heart.

This is way beyond my abilities. However, I asked for wisdom to do this work. I believe that you will sense God's presence and unction as He speaks to your heart while you read this book. I pray and believe that God will reveal to your heart and soul His Love and your ability to love. I pray that you will know that He has spoken through these words to you. He has spoken about removing all fragments of fear of loving again. This is from Him for you, without a doubt.

I believe that this book will greatly benefit those who have had numerous failed relationships or encounters, and those who may be married but didn't get off to the good start that we all assume just happens after saying "I do."

I would like to thank all who have prayed for me over and over in anticipation of this book and work. May patience reveal that it was worth the wait? May this book be a fruitful tool in the future lives of so many who desire to love and be loved by becoming more loving, not just for a day but for a lifetime. As I say in my poem "The Force of Love," I hope you are reminded just how powerful Love is when we possess it and allow it to operate fully within our hearts and souls, because we are no longer afraid to Love.

From a popular sci-fi movie, I say with knowledge of what Love can do in your life: may the Force of Love be with you all.

    Pastor Tony K. Thomas
    John 13:34–35

Most people's love will grow cold.

—Jesus Christ

CHAPTER 1
A Sign of the Times

Jesus said in the gospel, "Because lawlessness is increased, most people's love will grow cold" (Matt. 24:12). Most translations say basically the same thing: wickedness, iniquity, and wrongdoing will increase, and many will withhold their Love.

I believe that we are living in these times. Love has become almost a distant trait. Most cannot remember when Love was real in their lives. Many have closed their hearts, minds, and lives to the idea or possibility of loving again.

I asked the Lord, soon after my divorce from a marriage of almost twenty years, not to allow my heart to become callous, cold, or closed. Also, I asked Him not to make me so single that I became selfish and self-seeking. I can say that He has answered those prayers. It hasn't been without going through many trials, but I still keep my faith in Him. We must remember a basic, universal, and spiritual law: *God is Love*. Love is the very being and nature of God. There is nothing wrong with Him or with Love. Love has never failed, nor can it fail or pass away at any time.

Jesus continued, "But the one who endures to the end, he will be saved" (Matt. 24:13). The word *endure* means to keep pressing on, to keep having faith, to keep trying. It means not giving up even when the pain is difficult to bear. *Endure* has synonyms like *last, live on, go on, survive, persist, continue, preserve,* and *remain*. So let's paraphrase the scripture as this: "But the one who keeps trying, pressing on, and continuing to love to the end, he will be saved."

We usually will read this as an end-time prophecy. However, I want to consider reading it as a message about Love in our times. It is a message for the end of times and a sign of the last days. I believe it is a principle that applies to our lives today.

We have to keep trusting and believing that God will provide. Living by faith will provide for our needs until the end of our days. Being saved is a product of endurance. Likewise, if we substitute *saved* for *love,* this passage reads: "But the one who keeps trying, not giving up, and having faith in Love until the end, he will be loved." This is just a play on words, but Jesus could be saying that you should never stop loving, no matter what, because God is Love.

In our lives, we will have numerous setbacks and pitfalls. God wants us to remain in faith and keep putting our trust in Him. As a reminder from Scripture, faith works only by Love. It doesn't work when we choose; it works all the time by Love. Love has never been weakened because of lawless acts or any wrong suffered. We cannot control what someone does, but we can control and minimize its effect upon our lives. God sees a new day waiting for all who put their trust in Him.

In the early days of the church, Christ warned that many false prophets would arise and lawlessness would increase. Put this in the context of Love and relationship-building. Many of us have experienced what we thought was the final Love, only to find it later revealed as a false alarm. We have to decide whether we will allow our hearts to become callous and full of dust, or whether we will continue to search for what is true and lasting in a loving relationship.

I believe that most people want to be loved and to give Love in return. Therefore, we have to recognize when we are faced with fear of Love, and to know that it is up to each one of us to do something about it.

Apostle Paul spoke of Love as the greatest of all and a lasting gift. When everything else has departed or failed, Love remains. Love doesn't keep reminding us of our past pains or hurts. Instead, Love provides the opportunity to hope and expect God's total gift of Love.

This is what my poem "The Force of Love" is about. I wrote it in early 2002. I didn't know that I would use it in a book on the subject.

I hope you agree that Love is still a gift from God. The reason I emphasize the word Love is because Love is God and God is Love. Love is that important a need and desire in our lives.

I find that many people no longer embrace the concept that Love exists for them. It's sort of peculiar that we question the existence of loving but seldom question our fear of loving. We think that we can predict and pick the times and ways that Love should come into our lives. However, the Creator of it all isn't on our timetable of scheduled events. "For My thoughts are not your thoughts, Nor are your ways My ways," declares the LORD (Isa. 55:18). Thank God for that.

God is Love. God has the great responsibility of matchmaking. Let's keep that responsibility with Him.

God loved us before we ever knew Him. He existed while we were lawless and full of iniquity. God knows that we have the opportunity to discover His great gift of Love.

> Sin will be rampant everywhere and will cool the love of many. (Matt. 24:12 TLB)

> For many others, the overwhelming spread of evil will do them in—nothing left of their love but a mound of ashes. (Matt. 24:12 MSG)

These are just a couple translations of this passage from the gospel of Matthew. Reading different versions of the Bible can illuminate the same Scripture passage with more meaning.

May you reflect upon the way Love is described as "cool" and "a mound of ashes." I believe that God has sent this book, *Why Are People Afraid of Love?* to do a work within the hearts of those who are longing to be loved before Love becomes as cold and lifeless as a mound of ashes.

So Why Are People Afraid of Love?

Many of us have prayed to discover lasting Love in our lives. I know I have prayed that prayer frequently. However, few expect that God will answer that prayer.

God is working on all our prayers right now. Let it be known that He doesn't need our assistance, just our trust and patience. Much asking doesn't change things with God. He has a bigger plan, and when it is revealed, it will bring us to our knees in gratitude.

Sometimes I think we forget just how far we may have drifted or what this fear of Love has done to our hearts and souls. Our Father has loving and gentle hands to shape us from mounds of ashes that have been blown by every wind of fear, so we can stand up again in His created Love. He desires that all people are saved. He also desires for us all to be loved. That should be without a doubt. He was the One who said in Genesis 2;16, "It is not good for man to be alone." He knows our desires and needs, but we must ask in faith. Scripture says "Faith only works by Love," "Faith expresses itself in Love" (Galatians 5:6, NAS, NLT).

So many people mask their loveless lives with things of this world, such as money, careers, friends, families, pets, and even church. However, we have to be honest within ourselves. Apostle Paul wrote in 1 Corinthians 13 that no matter what we accomplish, give, or possess, if we do not have Love, these other things are absolutely nothing. They are rubbish or "a mound of dust."

In my singleness journey, I have encouraged many people at various stages in their Love walk. It's sad to say that I have found few to be actually loving or even expecting to be loved. I have met some people who are empty vessels living without the power of life, which is *Love*.

Today, many people are afraid to say the word Love or feel the emotion. As Scripture says, their Love has cooled or become ashes. We think that if Love comes too soon, then something is wrong with it. If Love comes too late, then it must still not be real. We have forgotten that God is Love and Love comes from God. Remember that from dust we were created, and to ashes we shall return. I believe that God has to again breathe the breath of Love into our souls to turn those ashes into hot flames of Love.

Love has become for some a complicated, nonverbal, unemotional, nonphysical way of expression. We learn to live and do our best when it comes to loving someone. However, God's Word says, "Faith without works or action is dead" (James 2:26). What a sign of our times, when Love has become cold and full of dust like ashes. Love requires action; it isn't something that will just exist in a dormant atmosphere. Love has to be cultivated and nurtured like the flowers we plant. Love isn't haphazard or something we hope for. It is a result of our actions.

The book of James mentions that if we doubt, we will get nothing from God. We are like waves tossing in the sea with no stability against the winds of life. This is the way some people are in their Love lives: starting and stopping, up and down, in and out, never able to get stable or to find soundness in a real relationship that produces lasting Love.

We just don't know what we want or need. We ask God, but often we doubt that He can do it. We date, we expect, we suspect, but very seldom do new relationships make it further than our previous failed ones.

You may be thinking that this is sort of negative. Nope, this is reality, the plain and simple truth. I have a couple sayings: "Hurt can be a part of the search. Pain is in the plan for change." Rejection is nothing more than a momentary disappointment or light affliction. When we are aligning our lives with God's plans, we will eventually see the purpose for it all. This isn't a bad time. It can become a blessing when we recognize the hands of our Father doing His work. God is at work at all times to answer your requests, but those answers may not come according to your timetable or by your workings. Scriptures says that God is at work in our lives to will and to do for His good pleasure (Phil. 2:13). He is saving us from major setbacks that we can't see at this moment.

I think we often forget that we are in the process of salvation. Eternal life is secure. However, salvation isn't just for our spirits—it's for our souls. Inside our souls are our emotions, our will, and our intellect. Love is a part of all three of these areas of our souls.

I believe that discovering the Love of your life is a process that continues until it happens. Once Love comes, then we have to continue to do the work to keep it growing and lasting. Please don't rush past the last sentence. Read it again and again until it is part of your plan for keeping lasting Love in your life. Remember, it is the will of God that we continue to do the work of Love until the end comes.

Let's zoom in on these words of Jesus: "But the one who endures to the end, he will be saved" (Matt. 24:13). I like to use this verse in reference to a lasting Love in our lives. We must learn to endure when it comes to overcoming fear of Love. We have an enemy who doesn't want us to enjoy the full joy of God's Love in our lives. To endure means not to grow weary in doing good, for in due season you shall reap if you faint not, (see Gal. 6:9). Don't lose hope in doing good, no matter what society does. We need to remain vessels of Love. We need to be people who believe in and can still Love.

Be assured that the answer to your prayers will come as you continue to remove the fear of Love from your soul. You may find a portion of the answer in each person that you meet. In each relationship I found that developed and ended, I saw a purpose and reason that assisted me in becoming a more loving person. The end of a relationship is not the final chapter. It could very well be the opening to a new or perhaps a continuing wave of Love. We are going to have our share of ups and downs, but faith in God will keep us anchored.

We must endure when it comes to Love. We know that God is at work, and He uses others to get the necessary work done within our souls. This is why God uses loneliness to keep our focus on Him. During those times when we are alone, our souls are being renewed. These are not times to put up more walls or surround our lives with moats of vicious mental or emotional caricatures. These are times to relax and let the Spirit of God do His work within our souls.

This work is important part of receiving the answers to our prayers. God knows what we need even before we ask (Matt 6;8). This is the time when we can bend and be shaped to understand that He is at work for His purpose. The Bible states that we should let patience perfect the work, so we can be complete, lacking in nothing (see James 1:4).

As you recall, one of the definitions of *endure* is to suffer (something painful or difficult) patiently. This is one of the keys to my life—being patient. One of my favorite animals is a turtle. A turtle will stay on its path. It doesn't see any danger ahead. All it knows is where it is going. If you ever help one that you find in the road, never take it back where it was coming from. Take it on its way across the road, or it will simply start to cross again. It knows where it is headed in life.

Only God can see the ills and dangers ahead on our journey of singleness. From time to time, He picks us up. He never takes us back but moves us ahead in life. I have found in my season of singleness that God has removed people from my life. This never happens without the pains or difficulties of relationship breakup, but there is always confirmation. He reveals that this person isn't for my best; usually He lets me know early on in the relationship.

I believe that He has also revealed similar things in your relationships that didn't work out. I believe He showed you that the breakup was for your best.

God doesn't show me all, but simply speaks as Father. However, I seldom listen. I must say that I wish I listened better. I know that I am not alone in this. Many times, we let our emotional and intellectual reasoning usurp God's will in our lives.

God picks us up. Each time, we can feel the strength of His hands and the care from His Love as He repositions us ahead in life. He wants us to get His best. Once he sets us back on track, we need to listen to His unction more intently. We need to look beyond our previous failed relationships and learn what our part was in the failure. This can *only* be done with the mirror of life.

We have to keep searching deep within ourselves. When this look inside our own souls is done correctly, I believe our wants shall be manifested. However, fear of Love will keep us tossed by the waves of past failures, until we recognize that Love doesn't operate at all in fear. Perfect Love drives out all fears.

Fear comes from our adversary, Satan. We all know that there is no Love in him. There is no truth in Satan. God's Word tells us to speak the truth in Love (Eph. 4:14). We have to be honest with ourselves and learn that we had a part in every breakup and failed relationship. Many of us have never stopped to look into that mirror and see that there were really things that we could have done differently. However, we've never been taught to do any better. Therefore, we don't know what else we could have done when it comes to developing a lasting Love.

I believe that it is now time to equip ourselves with the tools, skills, and abilities to manage our fears of loving. We must endure until we get to where we are headed in life, especially when it comes to discovering Love.

Why are people afraid of love? Could it be that people have allowed the Enemy of mankind to plant his seeds of hopelessness, fear, and doubt deep into their souls? I have to ask: What do you want when it comes to Love? Do you want Love or not? Take a moment and write your answer down on the page of reflection at the end of this chapter.

Many people think that companionship, friendship, and fellowship can be had without a mission or purpose. I have heard many say that they are not ready for anything serious. Well, don't date. If you are afraid of the hurt, don't start the search. It is okay to stay on the sideline. If you step on the relationship playing field, you need to be ready to play the relationship game entirely. I mean, why get involved with another? Stay to yourself and stop complaining.

In my opinion, if you desire to date, then you desire to be loved. Love doesn't sit around waiting for anyone to activate it. Love is a powerful force, and it is action.

Remember that faith works by Love. Faith without works is dead.

Love is work. Without work, Love will die or become mounds of ashes. I don't care what stage you may be in in your Love life. There has to be some work performed to keep it working properly.

Love requires focus. We need to know where we are headed. We need to move forward, not backward. God is with each of us, and His hands will keep us from falling headlong.

> The steps of a man are established by the Lord,
> And He delights in his way.
> When he falls, he will not be hurled headlong,
> Because the Lord is the One who holds his hand. (Ps. 37:23–24)

REFLECTIONS FOR CHAPTER 1

Take the time and reflect upon the words from Chapter 1, look into your soul and determine where you are when it comes to love, if love has cooled, list ways that you can re-kindle the flame of love. Do you want Love or not? What do you want when it comes to Love?

Fear's breath can be smelly, but Love's breath is a sweet air freshener.
—Apostle Tony K. Thomas

CHAPTER 2

What Love Is

First, we have to learn what Love is and what Love isn't. We have to go to the very source of it all: God. No matter what you believe or don't believe, the universal and divine law is that God is Love. I know this may cut some readers, but it's the truth. God is Love. That is why Apostle Paul could write that Love never fails.

So often we see Love as some faraway promise in life. I have heard some say about Love, "If it happens, it happens." We have heard songs and movies speak of Love as something that isn't that important—for example, in titles like *What's Love Got to Do with It*. Likewise, I have heard people talk about relationships and never mention the word Love. However, Love is still Love and very much available.

It is important to know what Love is. Many times what we call Love, or think it is, isn't Love at all. Often, Love is not involved in our relationship-building process. We build it on activities, dinners, friends, or other associations, but not on the basis of Love. Knowing that God is Love, we should know that Love can endure any conflicts and will be giving at all times. Love suffers long; it isn't a habitual quitter.

We need to recognize the failures in our concepts and practices of Love. We need to seek the answers to why we are single and why we are still searching. The main reason is perhaps that we never learned our life lessons. Life is our best teacher, not our friends or family members. No one can see your pain or your need to change like God can. God desires to put you across the road, out of harm's way. Things are still in His hands and control.

God's protective services are always working. I call them my GPS. God's protection many times feels strange. It really does take some getting used to, but once you accept it—wow, life becomes so much more meaningful to live.

God knows the desires of our hearts. He simply wants them to line up with His will for our lives. He desires to give us our desires when the time is right. He knows that we need to grow and develop into His will for us. We finally mature when we have learned to put our trust in Him for all things.

Let's look at this Scripture passage. I have used it a lot in my life. Now I believe it even more:

> Delight yourself in the LORD;
> And He will give you the desires of your heart.
> Commit your way to the LORD,
> Trust also in Him, and *He will do it*. (Ps. 37:4–5, my emphasis)

God is light, life, and Love. God knows what He is doing and where He is guiding us. This one passage means so much more to me today. I have read it and quoted it many times in the last thirty-plus years. I know that I must trust in the Lord and commit it all to Him. Give it to God and let it remain with Him.

When we are afraid to love or be loved, we don't know God's will for us concerning a relationship. Personally, I have been at this place of fear numerous times. I am thankful today for GPS guiding me through these rough winds and dark clouds. Without God's guidance, we are wandering aimlessly, feeling our way through life.

We can be severely burdened by the fear of Love. We might, through luck, hit it off, but normally such relationships are short-lived. Today is the best time to begin to discover that a healthy Love life will always depend on you. I am glad that I recognized this and learned that I needed to deal daily with a nemesis in my life: fear. I refuse to personalize fear. We have all made reference at some time to "my fears." It is never too late to discover that fear has no business being in our lives on a permanent basis.

In the New Testament and as well as in life, Love and fear are opposites. They are in constant conflict and battle for our souls. We need to recognize the effects of each of these forces, especially when it comes to developing relationships. Fear causes our hearts to be closed; Love causes our hearts to be open. Fear does not come from God. Love comes from God above. Fear will repel while Love will attract.

It is important that you take the time to review God's Word. That is the only way to learn of the will of God. The Word will register in your soul, coming not from your thoughts or your environment but from the greater One. This is a way the Spirit of God guides us—by reminding us what God's Word says about particular subjects as these become relevant in our lives.

Right now, get your Bible and look up the following verse. Never assume that any author, including me, is correct. Look at your Bible and become familiar with what it says. It will become a resource and give you guidance when you pray and make life decisions. This is how GPS guides us in our singleness journey.

> For God hath not given us the spirit of fear; but of power, and of Love, and of a sound mind. (2 Tim. 1:7 KJV)

Please let this verse soak into your soul. Look at every word and slowly read it. God didn't give fear to you, so why do you accept any component of it?

We allow fear to govern much of our lives. I hope that readers will discover this lifelong truth. Fear isn't supposed to be dictating our lives. Discarding fear doesn't happen overnight; it happens when we are fed up and ready to grow. When you are down, there is only one way to go, and that is up, up, up!

Fear is tricky. Its roots are found in deceit, division, and destruction—the will of the Evil One. Fear will make you think you are over it, but it will keep rising again and again. Fear can't be a friend. Never receive advice from fear. Fear can only be an enemy, to stop you from advancing, accomplishing and even receiving, what is rightfully yours, which are power, Love, and a sound mind. *Wow*! Or WOW—I am walking on water.

No one can discover or obtain a lasting Love until they learn to master fear. Fear is a destroyer. Apostle John called it a tormentor, and it is just that, a tormentor. Fear prohibits us from obtaining the desires of our hearts. Let's look at John's description in two different versions of the Bible:

> There is no fear in Love; but perfect Love casteth out fear: because fear hath torment. He that feareth is not made perfect in Love. (1 John 4:18 KJV)

> There is no fear in Love [dread does not exist], but full-grown (complete, perfect) Love turns fear out of doors and expels every trace of terror! For fear brings with it the thought of punishment, and [so] he who is afraid has not reached the full maturity of Love [is not yet grown into Love's complete perfection]. (1 John 4:18 AMPC)

Again, take a moment and reread this. Let it soak deep into your spirit.

This passage is powerful and says a lot as to why people are afraid to love. Mainly, I believe that many don't know what Love is. Love requires us to grow, mature, and manage all fears that come against it.

I like what the Amplified says: "Love sets fear out of doors and expels every trace of terror." Fear can produce all sorts of mental anguish that becomes torment from within. Such torment soon manifests in a relationship.

One thing for certain is that fear is going to come. You can count on it. Fear doesn't mean something always seems wrong. It may falsely indicate that everything is all right. This is why I have written this book—to assist you in how to get beyond the surface. Learn to develop the lasting, maturing Love that will remove all fear. It takes skill, tools, and abilities on both parties' parts to go beyond the superficial "love" that each person may be used to experiencing. If each person in the relationship desires the opportunity to create something special and lasting, it will require a little bit of ingenuity and, most of all, Love. Love is a force, a power from above that flows freely for all who harvest its touch and assistance.

I discovered this passage of Scripture when I was married. During several marital arguments, I didn't have an answer other than the Word of God. I used this verse and often shared it. Little did I know that once the grip of fear has set in, it is not easily removed. Most of us will discover that many disagreements come from the fear of uncertainty. Love is the one force that can remove that fear.

Love will be tested, like any other gift given by God. I believe that fears are just the fine fibers used to fuel the fires that rise to the level that Love is required to handle.

We have all heard the term "falling in love." When we "fall in love," we can easily fall out. Therefore, we need to learn to grow together in Love. But there isn't any crystal ball other than our own hearts' desires. I tell you that if two people keep that burning desire to be one, nothing will pull them apart. This applies to both Christians and non-Christians.

It is the law of Love that perfect Love will cast out all fears. When all you hear coming from someone's words is fear, it is time to deal with it, immediately. Fear is real. It can manifest itself as being solid, though it is only speculation. Fear can paint a pretty good picture of doom and gloom and torment. Fear has one purpose, and that is to punish you. It will make sure you remember that punishment for the rest of your life. Fear is ruthless. It is a tormentor. It can divide the best of friends so that they never speak again. That is why people seldom recover from the heartache and pain of failed relationships.

I want to let you in on a secret: whatever fear says isn't reality. Reality is what is in God's Word. Jesus has given each believer authority over all the power of the enemy (Luke 10:19). Therefore, rise and stand up and be renewed.

I have to admit that fear can do a good job of selling its desires. Fear desires that we fail to grow or get past pain. That may seem like a real chokehold. Fear possesses the ability to make us think that it will win. Fear gets us to move before we can witness the force of Love.

I didn't know that God was using the stormy and rough times of my failed relationships to train me and prepare me for this work. I have felt the force of fear many times in my own singleness journey. I know it is real and what it can do. I have seen the face of fear in many faces. I've heard fear's voice speak in the words of those I have encountered. That is why the Lord has enlisted me to write this book. He knew that I would pay attention to the details of relationship-building.

Fear can be a major contributing factor in keeping a person from their heart's desires. When we are afraid of Love, then we can never obtain it. We can't even see it or know that Love is present. Love is far from fear, and fear is far from Love. Fear pushes us away from loving and in some cases from being loved.

Some people have never experienced the force of Love working to remove all fears. How can they? Many of our failed relationships end the same ol' ways for the same ol' reasons. We believe that those are the actual reasons for the relationship ending, but the same ol' reasons are seldom true.

We need to do a personal inventory and realize that we need to learn what true Love is. We have to admit that we only had an imitation of Love. Each one of us has been invited to Love, but not knowing what Love is has prohibited us from accepting the invitation.

Fear or Satan can masquerade as Love, but deep inside we will always question the validity of that masquerade. Satan knows what we are seeking. He doesn't know all, but he knows enough to hinder us and get us to abort the journey. Mainly, I think that we tell him too much. We do this in our complaints, self-talk, and thoughts.

During our down times, I believe that we talk more to the Devil than we do to God. Fear will remain until we stare it down and make a life-changing effort not just to speak against it, but to destroy it. Fear attacks your heart's desires. It has an unending track record for killing dreams, hopes, and lasting Love.

For most people, fear has become so normal that we treat it like one of our pets or an adopted child. We serve it instead of allowing it to serve us. Fear can serve us in a positive way. When we recognize fear and work to manage it, we practice a real lesson in growing and becoming more loving.

When I first separated from a marriage of nineteen and one-half years, I faced frustration when it came to communicating with another lady. They would say to me, "You are too good" or "You sound like you are seeking Ms. Perfect" or "I don't think I will be good enough for you."

Of course I gave attention to these words. I often wondered if they were right. I have only done to the best of my abilities what Scripture asks of each of us: to love God with all your heart, obey His commandments, and love your neighbor as yourself.

I got tired of hearing these words. It seemed that I wasn't getting to know anyone. I began to realize that perhaps it wasn't me, but the world of singleness that I had just entered— what the world calls "dog eat dog," "selfishness," and "I, me, mine" mentalities. Past pains were lingering on their faces and keeping most from going further than they had previously been in their Love lives.

I was thankful that, after spending almost half my life being married, I still believed in Love, and that singleness was my fresh start to discovering it. I possessed the energy and mind-set to make the next choice the right choice. This decision was the best decision for me.

Finally, I decided that what the ladies were saying to me was true. I was too good, and I was seeking the perfect lady for me. I wondered how each woman could know so early in our conversations that she was not the one for me. We really didn't know one another. But they knew themselves.

I had to learn that people will tell you where they are in life and where they are headed if you choose to listen. I didn't listen at first. Instead I sought to prove them wrong. I would get involved. Then a light bulb would come on inside my soul, and I could see clearly the path they were on, what they were saying, and why. This happened to me time after time along this journey of singleness.

I knew deep inside that God's Spirit was speaking to me and guiding me in each of these encounters. However, like so many of us, I ignored Him. God is merciful and full of loving-kindness. Each time, He stepped in and made things plain to me. I would be deeply involved, emotionally as well as in other ways. One expects to be so in a relationship. However, I knew that God was speaking to me and I had to obey. This is never easy but is always necessary, especially when you can see the deceit and trickery of the Enemy that allows someone to not walk in the uprightness of their own heart. There were times when God had to simply remove someone from my path, mainly by telling them to let me go.

At first, these events felt strange. But once I could see the Lord's purpose, I felt a special Love from my heavenly Father. After several relationships ended the same way, I realized this wasn't some coincidence. It had a purpose and was perhaps planned or even ordained.

I truly believe that many of you have had similar experiences. I found that God was moving me from past mistakes, pain, and weakness into becoming a real king. He wasn't taking me backward but forward and higher. He placed me across the road and encouraged me to continue my journey of singleness with His guidance. God's protective service (GPS) was working for me, even when I wasn't paying it any attention.

That is the way our Father is. He loves at all times. I didn't know that He was preparing me to be a king—one who is strong, who rules well, and who makes right decisions in life. The ladies who came across my path were directed and guided by my Father. Each encounter was lifting me out of despair and weariness that I didn't even know existed within my soul from my past relationship failures.

What Is Love?

Even at this time, the Holy Spirit is teaching me and showing me more about this subject. We saw in 1 John 4:18 that perfect Love casts out all fears. Now let's look at a few statements that come before that verse. "We have come to know and have believed the love which God has for us. God is love, and the one who abides in love abides in God, and God abides in him" (1 John 4:16).

I like that Apostle John says that we have come to know and have believed. This tells me that knowing and believing in the Love which God has given to us is a process, not just something that any of us get right away.

Apostle John tells us all that God is Love. He says this over and over, starting at verse 7 in chapter 4 of this first epistle credited to him. This is a powerful statement when we allow it to drip sweetly and deeply into our souls. Love is something that we need to live in or expect to be a part of our lives. Love doesn't just happen. Love exists in all who abide in God. It is impossible to be a Christian and not possess the essence of Love.

Therefore, as believers, we should always know that Love isn't just available, Love is possible. The one who walks in Love walks with God's guidance; God will walk with them. God is our GPS and desires each of us to possess Love in our lives.

The apostle continues, "By this, love is perfected with us, so that we may have confidence in the Day of Judgment; because as He is, so also are we in this world" (1 John 4:17). It is an amazing discovery, at this stage in my life, to learn that by knowing that God is Love, this is what will perfect Love with us all.

Some may wonder what God has to do with this. God has everything to do with Love. He should have everything to do with our loving and our choices. However, Judgment Day will always come. I call this the time of testing, and it will come. It comes to push us back and question the Love that has just arrived within our thoughts and hearts. It's like something is there but we can't quite define it. We feel it and think it, but we don't know what it is. We have conditioned ourselves to agree with fear instead of with Love. Glimpses from the past or negative thoughts from within become more powerful than the All-Powerful One, the All-Knowing One, the Ever-Present One—the Love that comes from God.

Think about this. By this, we are perfected in Love. The "this" that the verse is referring to is nothing more than knowing that Love is God and God is Love. Knowing this gives us confidence when the time of testing comes.

Receive this Scripture passage as a guide to relationship-building. Place it in your heart's tool kit to repair and restore your soul.

The confidence that we have should be simple for a believer. However, it is far from simple. It may take some serious effort to learn the benefits of knowing that God is Love. The main benefit is that if God is Love, you are Love or you can love. For as He is, so are we in this world. This all takes practice. Practice doesn't make things perfect, but practice can assist in making things better over time.

John's statement alone should set some people free from their fears, from their reluctance to push past their pain. The world can affect us because it's an environment of dog eat dog and an eye for an eye. When it comes to loving, we should seek glory begetting glory and gentle mercy.

We are the creatures and God is the Creator. His Word is our guide to conduct and should form our thoughts. As He is, so should we be in this world. No matter what happens, we need to know that we are not to succumb to the effects of the world around us. We are to present our best and leave it at that.

Learn to turn what-ifs into why-nots. I had to learn after many years of starting and stopping relationships at the same ol' place and finding or making up the same ol' excuses for it. One day I recognized that I'd had the answer with me all along. The Spirit of the Lord directed me to look at my name, Tony. He impressed upon me to spell it backward, so I did. When you use the letters from my name backward, you get YNOT—why not.

There are times when the Spirit of the Lord makes you feel small as you learn how He is with you. He was letting me know that I had the power to move beyond the Day of Judgment that comes when Love begins to develop within our souls.

Now read 1 John 4:18. I hope this time something will burst inside your mind, like an alarm sounding to say, "It's over." The judgment has come and gone, and I am still standing. Now I stand in the confidence of knowing that I still believe in Love. I can love as many times as it takes until the final Love comes. "There is no fear in love; but perfect love casts out fear, because fear involves punishment, and the one who fears is not perfected in love" (1 John 4:18).

Now we can say God is Love and Love is God. We can say, "There is no fear in God." I hope you can let this verse be a springboard in your tool kit of learning to develop Love by moving beyond the fear that will come. May it be a foundation that you can build from and allow to reset your Love life.

Remember: old things and ways of thinking will pass away, and new ways of thinking about loving will arise.

What is Love? Love knows that God is everything. He is truly in our lives, to love and teach us all how to be Love for another. Apostle John gave us the key in the next verse. Take a moment and let this verse speak to your soul. See it as our heavenly Father sees you and me. He sees us as an extension of His Love because, as He is in this world, so are we. "We love, because He first loved us" (1 John 4:19).

Love is God, and God's Love will teach us and guide us to love as He has loved each of us. You can do this in every encounter and relationship opportunity that comes across your path. The energy to resist, reject, and question Love is the same power it takes to receive, rejoice, and be rewarded in knowing that God is allowing another opportunity for Love to be developed.

Remember, Love isn't what we go out to seek. It is what we enable ourselves to become. When we possess Love's power, we know that nothing can keep us from becoming more loving, lovable, and in Love.

Love is God and God is Love. Knowing this will keep our focus not on the way things are, but on what they should be and can become.

God is real and Love is real. God wants us to know that Love is His ultimate gift. He loved us before we first loved Him.

What is Love? Love is the ultimate gift from God for each of us to share and give to one another. So *why not* push past the thin walls of fear and discover this wonderful gift? It will be a gift that keeps giving forever.

Perfect Love is the knock-out punch

LOVE

There are many types of Love
All are needed to become whole
Mankind has always tried
To possess them all

There is a Love to just be accepted
A sense of warmth that flows
From being a part of a group
And feeling that there you belong

Also, Love is security
Safety from not being alone
Time taken up with pleasure
Bringing joy for our souls

Love is commanded by God
That we should share together
Never seeking our own desires
But willing to sacrifice for another

Love will set you free
While for some it seems hard to find
Love will cast out all fears
Perfect Love is real

Love is free
But it seems to cost so much
Many are not willing to let go of it
Because they fear being hurt

Love isn't selfish
It doesn't seek its own
Why do you give, seeking a return?
You haven't given but only loaned

Love is patient and kind
It's not jealous, conceited, or proud
Nor a dream, fantasy, or speech
Love is action and can be felt

Love never gives up
It will seek an entrance
You hold the rights of passage
Will you let it in?

Love is the greatest
It's worth letting in
Love can't be purchased
It is always owed

Then one can reap the harvest
Enjoy the fruits from its fields
For Love needs no soils
Just needs to be planted

In a good heart
That will nurture it
And allow it to mature
To be given to another

The ultimate gift given
That comes from the Father of life
To those who will receive it
Love

Priceless Production

REFLECTIONS FOR CHAPTER 2

During this time of reflection from Chapter 2, list the things that you thought love was when it wasn't love. Also, list what love is and should be in your life, so that you will recognize it when it appears in another's life. Can you recognize some of the traits of fear in your former relationships that kept you from receiving or giving Love?

A king who is afraid of Love is a pauper.

—Apostle Tony K. Thomas

CHAPTER 3
Move Forth and Say No More

After a few years of dating, I spoke with someone via an internet chat room, instant messaging, and telephone. I believe that this lady could have been an angel. I never met her in person; she was from Alexandria, Virginia. She was a Hungarian Jewish Christian. We spoke a few times. She recognized my concerns about dating and loving again, and she challenged me to bring them all to God and tell Him what I desired. For the purpose of this book, I will call her Vivian.

Vivian said to me, "Tony, you do not know what you want." This was a bit confrontational and shocking to me, but I knew that she was mostly right. I did know what I wanted, but I was afraid to say it because of my fears and past hurts and pain.

I find that we often pray the same prayers or have the same thoughts when it comes to what we really want God to do for us. Those desires become front and center among the thoughts that are within our souls as we approach the throne of grace. However, when we are afraid, we seldom make these thoughts or desires known to God. Instead we mask them over and hide them deep inside, as if God won't see them.

I had to admit that my heart's desire was for a soul mate, but I couldn't say the word *wife*. The words *wife* and *commitment* and *relationship* were forbidden to cross my lips. Even so, I was seeking God for exactly that which in my soul was forbidden because of fear and pain. I know this sounds counterintuitive. Well, it is.

This is just another reason why people are afraid of Love. We don't know what we really want. I believe there are many others who have the same contradictory thoughts I had. I am not alone in this matter, or am I alone on this journey. Most people that I have met were in the same boat that I was. They would make known what their desires were, but they had done very little to prepare themselves for fulfillment of those desires. They were counting on other people to be suited to them, while they themselves seldom changed. Instead of improving our relationship skills, we simply continue doing as we always have and mask over the real person inside.

When I last spoke to Vivian, it was New Year's Eve 2003. I had been divorced for approximately one year at that time, but the divorce process had taken a couple of years. My New Year's tradition as a pastor is to attend an evening worship service. The service starts around nine o'clock and runs until after midnight.

Once a year, the Spirit of the Lord impresses upon me a prophetic word and message for the body of Christ. That year's message was "Move forth and say no more in 2004." As I am writing this now, I realize I was giving myself an opportunity to move beyond where I had been on my journey of singleness.

The service ended around one o'clock in the morning. I live over an hour's drive from the church. As I drove home, I called several friends to wish them a happy new year. Then I stopped by the Waffle House in Morrisville, North Carolina, near the Raleigh-Durham airport, around three o'clock. The words of Vivian came into my spirit: "Tony, tonight when you pray, why not simply tell God what you want?"

When I got home around four thirty, I got on my knees, and I begin to pray and seek the Lord. I felt as if I was taken instantly into the throne room of God, into His very presence. I heard from within my spirit these words: "Son, what do you want?" I had never felt such a knowing. At that very moment, I had no doubt that whatever I asked for would be given to me.

I am no novice in seeking the Lord. I have learned through the years how to get to that place of answered prayer. Instantaneously, what came into my spirit was that I could ask for any amount of money or any woman or any goal in life. At that time I had crushes on Halle Berry and Condi Rice. Can you imagine asking the heavenly Father for one of those fine ladies and sensing that He would grant your request because of your spiritual connection?

But my response to God was the honest truth. Even at that time, I could not pray for a wife, though that was in my heart and thoughts with every breath.

I hope that you can see that our heavenly Father knows all things. He knows what we need even before we ask. The grip of fear doesn't leave us because we pray. It's right there with us.

While I was in that special moment of His divine presence, I simply said, "I don't know, Lord, but I want Your will to be done." His presence left me, and my prayer was over. I was simply on my knees beside my bed. I crawled into bed and went to sleep. I didn't know that I had begun to move forth. It was my first step in learning to say no more. Wow!

The next morning, I awoke around seven thirty. I felt as if someone had punched or kicked me in the side. The Spirit of God impressed upon me to get my Bible. Now, waking up groggy from a few hours of sleep, who knows where their Bible is?

I have a number of Bibles. There's one in almost every room in my house. However, God didn't mean just any Bible. He wanted me to get my Amplified Bible. It was like a bright light was shining across the room to direct me to where that Bible was located. My Amplified Bible was underneath a pile of paper on the computer printer stand.

I walked across the room and got that Bible. Then I sat up in my bed and opened it. It was like my Bible was in sync with the voice in my spirit. My Bible opened to Proverbs chapter 31. The Spirit of God guided me to read the first verse. I heard the voice from within my heart say to me, "From now on, son, you are a king." I was a king made by the King of Kings and Lords of Lords.

I want you to know that this was truly a "move forth and say no more" experience. So often we miss what is within our reach because we are blinded by fear, pain, and misery. As I write, I am having a fresh God moment by realizing that the very Word that He impressed upon me for the body of Christ then was a true word that continues to guide me today. "Move forth and say no more." It opened a door, and it's an invitation for us all to move forth and enter in. This reminds me of Psalm 24:

> Lift up your heads, O gates,
> And be lifted up, O ancient doors,

> That the King of glory may come in!
> Who is the King of glory?
> The LORD strong and mighty,
> The LORD mighty in battle.
> Lift up your heads, O gates,
> And lift *them* up, O ancient doors,
> That the King of glory may come in!
> Who is this King of glory?
> The LORD of hosts,
> He is the King of glory. (Ps. 24:7–10)

I wonder how many doors or opportunities each of us have missed because we didn't look to the help that is above us. The King of Glory knows all things and sees all things. He has done so since long before you or I got to where we are today. We see things as closed; He sees things as open and about to change. I believe that was where I was on that New Year's Eve—at a place where God wanted me to be; a place where I could once again lift up my head and see the open door of hope and love.

This door is ancient because it was always there. The door is a real place, through which we can enter and commune with our heavenly Father. This may be the entrance into something that you never noticed before or couldn't see until this time. All I know is that when the King of Glory steps through the door we have opened, He will come in. He will come in with the fullness of who He is. He will come in with the answer, not just a quick fix.

I can now see that He stepped through that open door which my circumstances had created—a door of need for Him. I came to prayer that night to bring my heart's desire to the Lord of Hosts. The Spirit of the Lord implanted within my soul a true word for His church and for myself: "Move forth and say no more."

This is why I am here, delivering an opportunity to look up beyond your fears and failures and allow the King of Glory to come into your situation. This is huge step, but a lasting experience that you will never forget.

There is power when we can move beyond where we are in mind and spirit. We've got to move forth. We've got to know in our hearts that we want a change, not just a temporary fix. It's when you move forth that God moves for you.

Scripture teaches us to draw near to God and He will draw near to us. Even though fear from past pain was with me when I prayed, my heavenly Father saw me resisting it by coming to Him for counsel and help. I was submitting to Him my desire to learn of His will for me. I didn't know it at the time, but moving forth and saying no more is the beginning of resisting and removing the fear of our past experiences from our souls.

It's amazing, the grace that comes from our heavenly Father. Grace has been given for each of our innumerable situations in life. Grace is God's power given for you to be able to do what you could not do without His assistance.

Even in this divine moment, I was being philosophical. When I couldn't ask for what I really desired in my heart that night, I said what I thought would sound good to God: "I don't know, Lord, but I want Your will to be done." God, in His infinite wisdom, took my fears and turned them into a mission. What a gift He delivered to me by His grace. I didn't know that He would begin to reveal to me—not in a day, but along the journey of singleness—what His will is for me concerning being single. In a way, that night in prayer, I had begun to move forth and say no more.

Now, let's continue with what the Lord of Hosts delivered unto me on the morning of that New Year's Day. There is no better way to kick off a new year than to be guided by the Holy Spirit of promise. I knew that this time wasn't just an open door for me, but for whosoever would come and seek His will for their situations. Remember, the Spirit impressed upon me to open my Bible to Proverbs 31 and begin to read.

Proverbs 31 begins, "The words of Lemuel king of Massa, which his mother taught him" (v. 1).

I had read this chapter in the book of Proverbs many times, but I had never actually started with verse 1. Normally when we read Scripture, we read the popular verses that we have heard many times before. However, that particular morning, the Spirit wanted me to see something about this passage that gets overlooked.

I had been taught that this chapter was a chapter *for women*. This time the Spirit led me to begin at the beginning of the chapter. I now know that it is a chapter for both men *and* women. The Lord knew what He was saying when He commanded me to be a king. He had given me a crown. Wow! It's the same crown that, one day, I will return to Him when I bow before Him.

Why Are People Afraid of Love?

This realization occurred on January 1, 2004. As I write this, it is late summer 2018. I still have not gotten comfortable with saying that I am a king or with being a king. However, I am learning that Scripture speaks of kingship way beyond those who are made rulers by human beings. I came to God to get an answer for what I wanted. What I received was an open door for the King of Glory to come into my desires.

However, I have to say that God doesn't wait on us. He speaks and it exists. Eight years later, in late summer 2012, God gave me another piece to this lesson in life. I don't know why, but part of my biblical study is to do word and names research. I decide to look up the meaning of the name Lemuel. I found it simply means "of God."

This is a key. The Lord had told me that I was supposed to call myself a king from now on, and this name confirmed it: a king of God. "Wow!" I shouted. "Hallelujah!"

I know that the world has coined the phrase that we are all kings and queens. No, no, no. You have to be made a king by the hand of God. There aren't magic beans or words, but a choice to make. You must accept being instructed and prepared for kingship by the King of Kings and Lord of Lords.

I am glad this part was hidden from me until that time. Now I can see and understand that God did speak, and He was true to His word. It has been and continues to be an amazing journey to see the hand of God guiding us to where He desires. I still stand in awe when I think that He called me *"a king of God."*

Remember, on January 1, 2004, the Spirit of the Lord spoke to me within my spirit and told me that from then on, I was a king. This was, for me, truly a time to move forth and say no more. It was a day that I will never forget. Even today, God is still teaching me about being a king. It hasn't been comfortable. However, when you have been made a king by the King of Kings, it is about how He sees you and not about how you see yourself.

What I have noticed about being a king is that I am aware of things beforehand that others seem either to ignore or not to see. I found out why:

> The king's heart is *like* channels of water in the hand of the LORD;
> He turns it wherever He wishes. (Prov. 21:1)

I had to learn after many relationships that I was protected. I gave my heart easily to anyone who took notice of me. Mainly, I think it was because I so much desired to be Love and to love. This happens often when we are recovering from past pain or relationship failures. The world calls this the rebound effect.

Everything would go fine for a while. Then, sometime later, my eyes would be opened. Bingo, I could see things that I had never noticed before. I could see that this person wasn't the right woman for me nor was I the right man for her.

God protected me again and again. One day, He said to me within my soul that my heart was being taken from me and put in a safe place—in heaven, because I didn't know what to do with it.

At times, I would say this to someone, but they always thought I was on some spiritual kick. I knew it to be true. God has my heart even to this day, for the heart of a king is in the hand of the Lord. This became the scriptural description of me and my search for the Love of my life. God knows our fears. He understands how to get us to push past them and step through the door of faith that works by Love.

This brings me once again to the great question, "Why are people afraid of Love?"

One reason is they seldom research it to find out what is beyond where they are. They seldom step through that open door of opportunity and discover what Love is. I can't count the number of times I have heard someone say, "I am afraid of falling in love and being hurt again." I know that place familiarly because I was once one of them. I can see their walls still standing that will prohibit Love from being received and given.

Love isn't falling or failing. When Love comes from God, it *can never fail*. Some people don't find true Love because what they have experienced as Love wasn't Love at all. It was just their definition of what they thought Love was.

Love isn't hidden or hard to find. We are just too afraid to go beyond where we have been and learn what Love really is. Perhaps it is time for you to move forth and begin to say no more. Stop verbalizing your pain and sorrow and move into a new place—a place where God desires to place you.

I believe this book can be a key to place into that door of opportunity and open it, so the King of Glory can come into your circumstances with regard to loving again.

We have looked at verse 1 in Proverbs 21. Now let's look at verse 2:

> Every man's way is right in his own eyes,
> But the LORD weighs the hearts. (Prov. 21:2)

A king will follow his heart and recognize that it is in the hands of the King of Glory. God turns his heart where He wants it to go. Yet waters without some form of control will cut their own path, and not much can stop them. The king's heart is as a river of waters that isn't just running wild but is guided with control by the hand of God.

As a civil engineer and professional land surveyor, I know what water can do. It is exciting to know that during the time of God's guidance, we learn that we have grown and are developing into someone who begins to know what Love is and what Love is not. Fear weakens its grip, and we can see there is a light shining. A door is open to allow Love to come in.

That morning was my open door. I began to move forth and away from fear. There is a day coming for you to do the same.

Notice that God didn't speak to my concern or to my heart's intent. He spoke to who I was. No matter what I faced, it didn't change me or define who I really was—a king of God. We all possess fear of loving again, but once we give this to our Father, He can guide us into the safe waters of recovery and discovery.

A king knows not to trust his own ways but to trust in the Lord's ways at all times. Kings of God do exist; however, few are prepared when they meet one. Therefore, why not become one? Give your heart to God and let Him guide you through that open door to where Love exists and fear is cast outside.

A king's Love is from above. It has already been tested and tried by the hand of God. This is a time to be prepared. Get ready, for Love has been waiting for you to walk past that fear. I am hoping that this book will assist you in the preparation for a lasting Love created by the Father above. Are you ready for Love?

THE LOVE

More than a word spoken
More than feelings showing
More than the time spent
Is the Love that we have

Like a new day beginning
A new world created
It is fresh and founded
Within our hearts

Not just a kiss
Nor a hand held tight
Not just in our heads
Nor dreams in the night

The Love is real
Not just something you hear
When circumstances change
Love still is there

Real Love can handle
Almost anything
It's not made to fail
But to endure forever

The Love from God
That He gives to us
What a gift, what a treasure
We both now know

So let us share it
Speak it continuously
So that it will sink
Down in our souls so deep

I love you
You are the Love
I have searched so long
And found it to be
In you

Priceless Production

REFLECTIONS FOR CHAPTER 3

Take the time to pray and write down the things that this Chapter has revealed to you about love. Are you ready to push past your fears into the open door of opportunity? Why not take the time and pray and tell the Lord what you really want to receive from Him when it comes to love. Be ready to listen to write down His response to your petition.

We are as we eat, drink, and breathe. We become as we see, think, and believe.

—Apostle Tony K. Thomas

CHAPTER 4
Our Upbringing

I think most of us can agree that how we were raised and what we were exposed to is important when it comes to our initial development of what we define as a relationship. Let's go back to Proverbs 31. It begins by acknowledging that these are words of wisdom from the life of King Lemuel: "Words of King Lemuel, the Oracle which his mother taught him" (Prov. 31:1).

The book was given to teach kings how to select a woman as a wife and the importance of making the right selection. It was given to King Lemuel, or king of God, by his mother. Our mothers are normally our closest and initial teachers in what to expect out of a relationship.

The first verse is a powerful key and is many times overlooked. This is where it begins for us all. God uses our mothers to teach us how to make good choices in life, especially when it comes to relationships. Mothers are vital in sharing their wisdom with us. I believe Scripture uses this to bring us back to our upbringing. How were we taught about Love and relationship-building?

I remember seeing my mother standing at the kitchen sink when I was a small child, before school age. She would tell me about what type of lady to choose when I came of age. She would say things like, "Don't go where ladies are loose or fast" or "Don't go where they don't have good home structure." She advised me to make sure that my chosen lady could keep up a house, cook, and clean. She should also go to church.

I imagine this might have been how King Lemuel, a king of God, remembered his mother's teaching. The Spirit of God has brought these things back to my remembrance. My own mother said to me basically what Lemuel's mother said to him: "Don't give thy strength to women or do the thing that destroys kings" (Prov. 31:3).

In other translations, that advice reads this way:

> Don't spend all your energy on sex and all your money on women; they have destroyed kings. (Prov. 31:3 GNT)

> Don't dissipate your virility on fortune-hunting women, promiscuous women who shipwreck leaders. (Prov. 31:3 MSG)

I believe that this passage is simply saying, "Don't waste your life on loose living for your own pleasures and loose women who seek you only for what you possess."

I never saw this before in these terms. I always was thinking of it from a sexual point of view, but it is much more than that. It is like what we read about in tabloids or witness in some Hollywood movies—a life used for self-gratification. Life can be wasted on foolish living when a person is not preparing to be a king of God.

There are biblical instructions available to describe who God would choose for you as a potential mate. Why not ask Him? This concept goes for both men and women. Ladies need to avoid men who are loose as well. In Christ there is neither male nor female; we are all one and a kingdom of priests and kings unto our God.

Many people did not witness a healthy and lasting Love during their upbringing. Many witnessed enduring Love that just remained for whatever the reasons. I happened to be one of them. I was brought up in a two-parent home, but my parents never had any teaching on how to be a husband or a wife. They learned by observing what was presented to them. Therefore, they passed down to me and my siblings what they had observed. I witnessed their enduring Love, but I seldom saw the practice of Love that would have been a great benefit in my life. That was the norm for my generation in the community I was brought up in.

Race wasn't a factor, nor which part of town you lived in. It was the way things were done. I rarely recall hearing a sermon about family or marriage in the church I was raised in or any other church in my area. The home was seemed to be off-limits to any words from the pulpits. The congregation would have called that meddling or not part of God's plan for the church. I don't think anyone realized that the images being etched into the hearts of children from dysfunctional homes would become a contributing factor in future divorce rates.

This reminds me of a passage from Exodus, when Moses had just given the congregation of Israel the commandments of God: "You shall not worship them or serve them; for I, the LORD your God, am a jealous God, visiting the iniquity of the fathers on the children, on the third and the fourth generations of those who hate Me, but showing lovingkindness to thousands, to those who love Me and keep My commandments" (Exod. 20:5–6).

We are all byproducts of the way we were raised. I have listened to many stories when getting to know people. I ask each person about their family situations. Many didn't have a two-parent home. Others were raised by a close relative, or even in a foster care system. There are many scenarios when it comes to family structure and upbringing. Each creates a different first impression of adulthood and attracting Love into our lives.

Today, when we start our search for Love, most potential partners in our pool of selections have seen relationships dissolve before they ever experienced any true or developed connection. They have experienced the pain and despair of a breakup or divorce, or the effects of others' unhealthy relationships. No one is perfect. We all can use a little assistance from more than our usual crowd of back-patters. You know, those who celebrate our brokenness by saying they are there for us and they know that we will be there for them when their turn comes. There is a wise old saying that "misery loves company."

The repetitive cycle can be a result of not coming to God for wisdom. If we seek Him for wisdom, we shall receive wisdom. He gives liberally and freely to all who ask. He is still a parent who can show us how to grow up and get beyond where we have been. Whatever kind of home or upbringing we may have experienced, God is our Father. We can get the best guidance from digging deeper into His Word and presence. There should be no doubt that God is Love.

I want to emphasize that even in the homes where Christian values are taught and in the church fellowship, many still witness broken vows and lack of the workings of Love. Therefore, we all need to dig deeper, seek the King of Glory, and let Him into our Love lives.

God's house is a house of order, safety, soundness, structure, security, and stability. Few people ever seek His guidance on how to conduct ourselves when it comes to Love, loving, and being lovable. There are many passages in the Word of God concerning dating, mating, and managing a loving, enduring, and healthy relationship. Much of this will be in my upcoming book, *Love School*. I want to say here that only God can change our image of Love. Only God can remove the tentacles of fear that have attached themselves to our souls because of what we witnessed and suffered from the dysfunctionality of our upbringing.

Our upbringing is real and can be uncomfortable to remember, but it plays a major part in the development of Love within our lives. So often we become, as Moses wrote, a byproduct of the failures that we witnessed. We become a chip off the old block. However, we are to be as the Rock on which we stand—unshakable, resisting the fears from past pain and failure.

Discovering what God has prepared for those whom He loves and who love Him is a start. It is time that we realize that we need to change. That is what the passage from Proverbs 31:3 did for me. I heard a voice from the past instructing me. God can instruct us in the way to go. So often when we think that we are ready to start over, we begin without God's guidance. When the Father guides us, it is time to sit down, listen, search, pray, and follow Him.

The season of singleness is a great time, but it may not be seen as such. I have recognized that loneliness can be a blessing and gift at a time like this. You can learn more about this period of singleness from my first book, *Loneliness: God's Gift to the Single*. This statement may seem boring and out of date, but when we humble ourselves before His mighty hand, it is rewarding and fulfilling. Humbling oneself takes a special person—one who doesn't just pray, but follows the ways of the Father. Remember, throughout the gospel, Jesus spoke often of the Father and shared what the Father taught Him.

God knows how to raise us even after the influence of our early environment and experiences. He knew that one day I would call upon

His name. He was waiting to reply with the answer that I had been avoiding. His Word is still working.

That New Year's morning, God simply spoke from within my heart: "Get your Amplified Bible." It was like time stopped. But life's Love lessons were beginning to be taught. Why not ask? Why not pray? Why not listen to the Spirit of Wisdom from above? God wants to share His precious promises and perfect gifts with you.

We all are candidates to become more loving and lovable people. But this work can't be done on your own initiative. The work must be done in the very presence of Love.

The Word of God says that He knows what we need even before we ask. "And when you are praying, do not use meaningless repetition as the Gentiles do, for they suppose that they will be heard for their many words. So do not be like them; for your Father knows what you need before you ask Him" (Matt. 6:7–8).

Take a moment during your personal reflection at the end of this chapter to ask the Spirit of the loving and living God to share with you. Ask Him to bring back to your remembrance anything from your upbringing that could be hindering you from growing and becoming more loving. So often, the Spirit points these things out, but we just don't take the time to bring them to Him.

There are reasons why someone will utter the words of fear, "I don't want to be hurt again." It is time to bring that fear and pain to the only One who can remove it. It is time to move forth and say no more. God doesn't go against anyone's will. He is not about force. He can reveal to us, but we have to be willing to give and trust Him with it all. Jesus is waiting for whosoever will come to Him for assistance. Jesus said: "Come to Me, all who are weary and heavy-laden, and I will give you rest. Take My yoke upon you and learn from Me, for I am gentle and humble in heart, and YOU WILL FIND REST FOR YOUR SOULS" (Matt. 11:28–29). We must come to Him.

You know the burdens you have borne as you have sought to discover Love in your life. We are members of the family of our heavenly Father. He wants to show each of us Love that will remove all fears and that is perfect, because it comes down from Him and not of ourselves. WOW—I am walking on water again, yes. We can only receive this Love when we keep our eyes on Jesus, not for a moment but for the rest of our Love lives.

The Spirit of God has taught me a lot about myself and how to remove the stumbling blocks from my soul. There is nothing like lessening the control of fear and beginning to walk in Love with all whom you encounter. Remember, everyone feels the fear and thinks about it. Fear is always going to be around. We just have to learn how to manage it and not allow it to dictate to us. This can only happen when you are serious about growing and going beyond where you have been. This is about you, not about anyone else. It's your time to do some real soul-searching and peek into the Father's house. Father knows best.

I have often said that I am nice because my parents raised me right and my heavenly Father has done the rest. God is the Father and knows how to discipline us. This is a supernatural work done by Him.

> You have not yet resisted to the point of shedding blood in your striving against sin;
> and you have forgotten the exhortation which is addressed to you as sons,
> "MY SON, DO NOT REGARD LIGHTLY THE DISCIPLINE OF THE LORD, NOR FAINT WHEN YOU ARE REPROVED BY HIM;
> FOR THOSE WHOM THE LORD LOVES HE DISCIPLINES, AND HE SCOURGES EVERY SON WHOM HE RECEIVES."
> It is for discipline that you endure; God deals with you as with sons; for what son is there whom *his* father does not discipline?
> But if you are without discipline, of which all have become partakers, then you are illegitimate children and not sons. (Heb. 12:4–8)

Perhaps the reason you may not have been able to discover lasting, enduring, and healthy Love is because you have been rejecting the guidance and discipline of the loving Father. I am so glad that this passage says whom the Father loves, He disciplines. We have to know that the times that doors were closed or tears fell weren't all bad. Possibly those times got us to draw near to our real home training that comes from above.

The Lord knows how to remove the tentacles of fear that have been there. Fear guides us away from Love. We seldom recognize and see that happening. We think it is the way things are supposed to be, or we simply put the blame on another. We attract where we are. When we are in pain, we attract more of the same and call it by a different name. We can all run from pain, but we will usually hook up with the wrong person for the wrong reason and in the wrong season. This kind of so-called love doesn't normally remain. It can become another arm of fear that will grip our hearts, souls, and minds and keep us from attracting the Love of our lives.

Some people equate Love with being hurt. Whenever I hear, "I don't want to be hurt anymore," I know that person is not ready, at that moment, for Love.

I recall being in the sixth grade and putting these words on the clipboard that held my papers for class: "Love is hate; hate is love."

My teacher saw that and called me to her desk as class was ending. She said, "Tony, why do you have that written on your clipboard?"

I was sort of embarrassed, but I spoke out, being only ten or eleven years old at the time. I said, "Because most of the time, the very same person that someone says they love seems to become someone they hate over time."

She tried to convince me that I was wrong and that I should remove the words from my clipboard. Yet I was speaking from what I had witnessed and therefore believed from my upbringing.

Now, if this was going on in my head at the early age, I believe there are others who can relate to this experience. Our upbringing is the first program that we receive about Love. Those words at that time were real to me.

But today, I can say they don't make sense. Why? Because, Love began to instruct me, that there is no hate or fear within its kingdom. I finally came to Him and found my burdens lifted. His discipline and lovingkindness are what enabled me to endure.

We can become what we see, think, and believe. I know that Love is in my future because I am growing, becoming, and attracting the Love that I have seen from my Father above. Love is God and God is Love. I think that He knows what it is all about. He is more than able to teach each one of us that Love does exist and that there is no fear in Love. Time, a person, or an emotion will not remove your fear or past pain. You must manage fear by coming to a loving Father and presenting your heart to Him for a change.

Why Are People Afraid of Love?

Let's go back to Proverbs 31:3: "Don't give thy strength to women or do the thing that destroys kings." Remember, these are words from a mother to her son. She is admonishing him. We don't know what Lemuel's age was. I think he was still a child or a very young teenager with a great future set before him. I believe that our future can be shaped earlier than we know. The mother in Scripture and especially in the book of Proverbs is usually the voice of wisdom. "Hear, my son, your father's instruction And do not forsake your mother's teaching" (Prov. 1:8).

I believe many people can benefit from having this voice of reason in their lives. Our Father is still giving us instruction today. He knows what we are and whose we are. We are the King's kids. We are to live our lives as kings of God and avoid the hidden dangers that have shipwrecked many leaders.

> Don't dissipate your virility on fortune-hunting women, promiscuous women who shipwreck leaders. (Prov. 31:3, MSG)

Even when single, we have to navigate in the vast waters of uncertainty in which we set sail.

Sometimes it looks like too many opportunities arise and we haven't given any thought to our destination. More and more people are afraid of Love and avoid the work that is required to prepare them for the commitment of a lifelong Love. Our mothers knew of these days, and I believe they have taught us or even prayed for us not to be shipwrecked by this freedom of singleness.

Those who are placed in our paths are there to teach us. They give us opportunity to navigate our lives by learning from the choices we make. Some opportunities look good, but underlying them are king-destroying reefs. The book of Jude describes them: "These are the men who are hidden reefs in your love feasts when they feast with you without fear, caring for themselves; clouds without water, carried along by winds; autumn trees without fruit, doubly dead, uprooted; wild waves of the sea, casting up their own shame like foam; wandering stars, for whom the black darkness has been reserved forever"

(Jude 12–13).

We all will encounter at least one relationship that fits Jude's description. We may encounter these kinds of romances during our journey of singleness, but we do not have to remain in them. We have to pick up our anchor and set out again into the troubled waters, knowing that we cannot remain in a place that will drive us away from our real Love. Our Love for God will once again fill our sails and do the necessary repair that will take us beyond this point.

We have to forsake our adolescent behaviors and know that the voice of maturity is for our protection. The voice of wisdom knows because she had to make the same decisions in her life. We are leaders, not followers. The place described in Jude is there to remove you from your destiny. We know better because we all have been trained in the palace of our God by listening to His Word.

Before I close this chapter, the Holy Spirit is bringing back to my memory a Love story. The love that I witnessed growing up wasn't the finished product of Love. What I saw in my later years wasn't the same as what I saw in my childhood. What I witnessed was Love enduring all things. Love lasted way beyond the thick and thin, richer and poorer, healthy and sick, and the good and not-so-good times. I witnessed the struggle of two people's decision to be together and love one another until death parted them. That is what Love is and what Love does: Love endures until the end.

I am proud to call this place home. Such an upbringing can only be understood through the lens of time. I saw that Love worked and it didn't fail. This wasn't only from my home but my entire community of aunts, uncles, cousins, and friends. The proof of that Love is in our community cemetery, where you will find spouses buried beside one another. What a testimony of Love. What a witness to the adaptations and provisions that Love provides.

I realize that if we only remember the past, we may never move forth through that open door of possibilities which only the future will reveal. The word *love* was seldom spoken in my home, but the acts of Love were shown. I saw two become one through their trials and tribulations. This was the result of their commitment to one another.

The Lord gave me a definition of Love a few years ago: "Love is simply a mutual agreement between two individuals to be committed to one another. When everything else changes, Love will remain because of their commitment." Today, I can say, if you want to know where I come from, go with me to my family grave site at the Seymour Cemetery in Moncure, North Carolina. There you will see my roots of Love.

What caused such a transformation? I believe it came from prayers that were prayed and lives that were surrendered to the Love of God by receiving Jesus Christ as their Lord and Savior. I remember praying and crying out to the Lord as a child, when difficult times came into the home. I prayed, "Lord, don't let my parents divorce."

Some years after giving my life to Christ, the Lord sent me home to save my family. I didn't know this would include seeing my very own parents accept the Love that comes from God into their lives. Christ's words are true: "But the one who endures to the end, he will be saved" (Matt. 24:13), even when the world's love has waxed cold. It is never too late to surrender your burdens to the Lord and learn of His comfort and rest for your soul.

Our upbringing may initially guide us in our reasoning, but the Word of God will renew our minds and lead us like a lighthouse to the safe channels of singleness. We know that we must follow the voice within our hearts that is placed there from heaven above. We will learn that God is protecting us and guiding us into a fruitful blessing of Love that isn't selfish.

Yet we must also know that we are lights, beacons on a hilltop, for others who journey across the waters of singleness. You might be just what another person needs to guide them out of those troubled waters of despair and hopelessness. Jesus said, "Let your light shine before men in such a way that they may see your good works, and glorify your Father who is in heaven" (Matt. 5:16).

Once we traveled beyond the time of our personal shipwrecks. Normally we can see that the glory of God was with us. This is a good time to give God the praise for saving us and keeping us from making decisions that weren't based upon good, sound reasoning. We are human, and many times our reasoning is based solely on the lust of the flesh, eyes, and the pride of life. Brothers and sisters in Christ, this is a work of the Spirit of grace. It is nothing less than miraculous when you know that you were shipwrecked, but now can see the process of restoration. It is a work that we all know could not be done on our own, but only by the hand of our loving Father who art in heaven. So let the King of Glory come into your heart, right where you are.

Love Lessons from Chapter 4

Jot down the ways Love was exemplified in your upbringing. Do you think this has influenced your definition of Love? Can you think of any former relationships that weren't fruitful? Can you now see there was a reason for those unfruitful moments?

Use the page of reflection and write them down. List what you learned from the voice that spoke to you from within your heart and by the Word of God. This is a good time to say the model prayer that Jesus gave each of us from our heavenly Father:

> Pray, then, in this way:
> "Our Father who is in heaven,
> Hallowed be Your name.
> Your kingdom come.
> Your will be done,
> On earth as it is in heaven.
> Give us this day our daily bread.
> And forgive us our debts, as we also have forgiven our debtors.
> And do not lead us into temptation, but deliver us from evil. [For Yours is the kingdom and the power and the glory forever. Amen."]
> For if you forgive others for their transgressions, your heavenly Father will also forgive you.
> But if you do not forgive others, then your Father will not forgive your transgressions. (Matt. 6:9–15)

It is time to forgive any and all people who have hurt you. Ask forgiveness from any whom you might have hurt in your past relationships. Move forth and say no more!

Thomas Family Home

REFLECTIONS FOR CHAPTER 4

Ask the Spirit of God to bring back to your remembrance anything from your upbringing that could be hindering you from growing and becoming more loving.

Never ever forget that God is Love and Love is from God.

—Apostle Tony K. Thomas

CHAPTER 5
Definition of Love

Again, let's ask the question, "Why are people afraid of Love?" Could it be that many have defined Love in their own way according to their own experiences? If that is the case, then it is their own definition of Love that they will seek, time after time, until they come to realize that they are just making a big circle in their journey of singleness. It takes a lot of humility to realize that perhaps one's definition of Love isn't correct or that one needs to ask for help in defining Love.

I hope that this book provides insight into defining Love, not in a literary way, but in a way that God has said in His Word, the Bible. I know that it takes a lot to swallow one's pride and get to this point of seeking help from our heavenly Father. Scripture speaks of how God resists the proud but draws near to the humble and give greater grace to the humble. Grace is what we all need when it comes to really seeking divine help.

I had no idea what Love was or how to discover it. I came to my senses eight years after a divorce. I never imagined in my wildest dreams that I would be one of the divorced members of my generation. I knew I was in love and that I loved and that I was lovable. It never crossed my mind that I didn't really know what Love was or even how to seek it.

After a number of failed attempts to discover Love, I realized that perhaps I wasn't alone in this dilemma. There had to be others in the same boat of repetitive starting and ending of relationships. I felt like Simon Peter when he stepped out of the boat that was providing him with momentary safety from the raging storm, and decided to go to where

Jesus was. Believe me, a storm is indeed raging—real, invisible forces that keep us in our comfort zone. You are not alone in this. Fear is a force and is felt by all. There is no one who hasn't heard its voice or felt it winds of opposition and resistance.

The difference happens when you decide to step out from behind your mental security blanket and begin the process of growing and going beyond where you have been before. You may at times feel alone in your courage to go, grow, and become more loving. Notice in Simon Peter's story that no one else even attempted to get out of the boat. They simply accept their fate. Simon Peter believed Jesus was his answer. He believed that as long as he kept his eyes on Christ, he could walk on water and through the storm.

However, when Simon Peter took his eyes off of Christ, he began to sink. Well, that was where I was—I was sinking in my walk of singleness because I was doing it on my own. I never asked for the Holy Spirit to guide me. I just thought that if I was good enough on the outside, I could handle what was occurring on the inside.

Well, I was wrong. Believe me; our Father knows where we are and what our intentions and purposes are. He knows that we will eventually call out to Him for help. Simon Peter began to sink, and so did I!

Amazingly, we don't cry out to God right away. We try to survive on our own. We try it again and again with someone else. But we still get to the same ol' place of sinking in all these broken relationships. The storms in our minds really blow. Our thoughts become our focus. Things like age, impatience, past hurts, anger, bitterness, un-forgiveness, hopelessness, and even despair can sink us.

There comes a time when we all will realize that we need help. Peter called out for help. I believe it was at his last breath. Similarly, I came to the throne room in prayer. It was not like any of my previous times of praying to God. I came torn and worn out from the effects of the journey of singleness. I had reached my last breath in prayer when it came to the relationship failures in my life.

This time, I simply said, "Help me. I need help." It was like all of heaven was waiting for me to get to that point of asking for divine assistance. This became my beckoning in almost every prayer that I prayed during that season. Jesus called this kind of prayer *babbling*—asking for the same ol' thing over and over. It's a sign that you may be drawing near to the point of letting go and resetting your focus on the Lord. When your prayers become frequent and repeat the same request, perhaps you have been focusing on the storm instead of the Lord. The Lord says, "Come to me." We all have to humble ourselves, get out of that boat of self-pity, and ask for our Father's help.

Again, it was like the Father knew that I would finally seek Him for guidance. I had to swallow my pride and self-righteousness to cry out for help. I didn't know what would happen, but I got up.

Then it was like I was starting school again. A fresh spirit filled my soul. I sensed that the Father knew I was ready to learn about Love. He knows how to answer our prayers:

> But you, when you pray, go into your inner room, close your door and pray to your Father who is in secret, and your Father who sees what is done in secret will reward you.
> And when you are praying, do not use meaningless repetition as the Gentiles do, for they suppose that they will be heard for their many words.
> So do not be like them; for your Father knows what you need before you ask Him. (Matt. 6:6–8)

I could tell that He decided to restore my soul, and this was the answer to my prayers. To be restored, renewed, and reset, we have to leave others behind. This is for you and your opportunity. So get ready to step out of that boat full of insecurities and false comforts that bring no changes in life. You can't be like those who are just staring at the fear of Love with no intention of overcoming. You can't stay in that boat of temporary safety with a crowd full of fear, hoping for the best outcome. You have to step out of your comfort zone and into the direction where the Spirit of God is leading you. Remember the story of Jesus and Peter walking on the water from Matthew 14, they all knew that Jesus was out there, standing on the water in the midst of the storm. Everyone in the boat heard Jesus say, "Take courage, It is I, do not be afraid."

Simon Peter was the only one to go further into the dialogue by saying, "Lord, tell me to come to you on the water."

"Come," the Lord replied.

It will always be a bit scary when we decide to come to Jesus with our concerns and cares. That kind of fear is a worthwhile feeling, because you are reverencing Jesus. The storms are real. Your imagination will run aimlessly until you set your sights upon Jesus in the midst of your storms. The storms or the fears can't shut Jesus up; you can hear Him speak to you even while in their midst.

He doesn't have to give you all the answers. One word will be enough to get you stepping toward Him who is your true ark of comfort and joy. Knowing that Jesus is standing and walking on the waters of your concerns should be enough assurance that everything is going to be all right. Your concerns are like solid ground to Him.

This is actually why I am writing these books. Just by hearing one word from the Lord, I chose to step out into the unknown of my singleness journey, to go beyond the storms of fear. I didn't know the depth of the storms that were raging within my soul and brought so much pain and fear of loving again. However, I knew that I was not alone and that there were many others who were in that same boat. So I stepped out and discovered that not only was the Father healing me, but He will use me to bring healing to others. As the Lord did for Joseph, what was meant for harm, He has turned into good for others during their season and journey of singleness.

Let's read in full and meditate on the story of Simon Peter walking on water with Jesus. See your personal storms, but decide to focus on Christ, no matter what your mind says or your eyes may see.

> Immediately He made the disciples get into the boat and go ahead of Him to the other side, while He sent the crowds away.
>
> After He had sent the crowds away, He went up on the mountain by Himself to pray; and when it was evening, He was there alone.

Definition of Love

But the boat was already a long distance from the land, battered by the waves; for the wind was contrary.

And in the fourth watch of the night He came to them, walking on the sea.

When the disciples saw Him walking on the sea, they were terrified, and said, "It is a ghost!" And they cried out in fear.

But immediately Jesus spoke to them, saying, "Take courage, it is I; do not be afraid."

Peter said to Him, "Lord, if it is You, command me to come to You on the water."

And He said, "Come!" And Peter got out of the boat, and walked on the water and came toward Jesus.

But seeing the wind, he became frightened, and beginning to sink, he cried out, "Lord, save me!"

Immediately Jesus stretched out His hand and took hold of him, and said to him, "You of little faith, why did you doubt?"

When they got into the boat, the wind stopped.

And those who were in the boat worshiped Him, saying, "You are certainly God's Son!" (Matt. 14:22–33)

Simon Peter did walk on water, but only when he kept his eyes and put his hands into Jesus's hand. Jesus is there to save us and to help us with the very things that we struggle with the most.

Once you step out of your comfort zone, you will notice that the concerns that kept you cringing didn't stop you from journeying further. Also, when you put the Lord into your concerns, their storms will subside.

Remember the start of the story? All were filled with fear. However, by the end they were in a safe place of worship. They discovered through their uncomfortable situation that God cared enough to send Jesus walking on water in the midst of the storm.

Our Love lives are important to God. You will find that Jesus is very near. Take note of that even when you begin to sink. Trust me: this is a walk of faith. You will stumble from time to time. All you have to do is cry out like Simon Peter, "Lord, save me!"

Remember that Jesus said, "But the one who endures to the end, he will be saved" (Matt 24:13).

We have to remain humble and continue to seek the Lord for comfort and strength. This journey isn't for the swift, but for those who put their trust in the Lord. Submit your Love life to Him. Resist the storms of fear and dread. Draw near to Him and He will draw near, and He will exalt you with the gift of Love.

> But He gives a greater grace. Therefore *it* says, "GOD IS OPPOSED TO THE PROUD, BUT GIVES GRACE TO THE HUMBLE."
>
> Submit therefore to God. Resist the devil and he will flee from you.
>
> Draw near to God and He will draw near to you. Cleanse your hands, you sinners; and purify your hearts, you double-minded.
>
> Be miserable and mourn and weep; let your laughter be turned into mourning and your joy to gloom.
>
> Humble yourselves in the presence of the Lord, and He will exalt you. (James 4:6–10)

Defining Love is the best place to start. This is a point when you are ready to listen to the Holy Spirit and to God, Who is Love, to speak of what He says Love is. It will take some humility and lots of self-reflection to know that we need a definition of Love that isn't limited to our expectations or experiences, but to what God says that it is.

Definition of Love

Love isn't things, objects, feelings, pleasures, charms, looks, money, stature, or status. Neither is Love a like or dislike. Those are choices. Love is a divine gift from God. *God is Love.* When we learn the true definition of Love, we realize that Love is a lot more. It is not distracted by what we thought it was.

The Lord gave me a definition of Love a while back. He revealed to me that "Love is simply a commitment between two people, not based on feelings, wealth, looks, or status." He also said, "When all other things change or cease, Love remains."

Right after my divorce in 2002, I went to God to discuss what I would do. I think this was a "tell God," not a "listen to God" type of conversation. I said to the Lord that I was going to get to know a woman as a man, but I would be kind, honest, and respectful to all, no matter what. God never said a word. However, He did impress upon me one thing—not to get involved into anyone's financial affairs or pay anyone's bills.

I didn't think much about this. Having been married for so long, I never had this concern. When I was married, we managed our finances together for our family's well-being. I had no idea about the single world I was about to enter. It had become lawless and Love had grown cold. As the song says, "What's Love Got to Do with It"? Many people we encounter equate Love to emotions, lust, and things. Many seek what you can do for them or determine Love by the things you do or don't do.

I did keep that one command from the Lord—not to pay anyone's bills or get involved with their finances. Many stopped talking to me or didn't start, because they believed that someone giving them financial assistance was an act of Love. They needed assistance long before they met me, and perhaps still do.

Love never comes down to our level. It has always been in the same place—with God. God is Love. God dwells above, not beneath. So what King Lemuel's mother told him is still pertinent today.

Don't give your strength to many women or do the things that will destroy a king. (Prov. 31:3, paraphrased)

Many people today validate their successes by having a number of women or men in their lives with no real goal for permanency. Fear will always keep one searching and seeking. However, a king knows that this will not advance his kingdom. A king of God realizes the true value of

Why Are People Afraid of Love?

Love. A king of God is not afraid of Love. He knows Love is essential to his life.

God has made you a king to know all things and to search all things out.

"It is the glory of God to conceal a thing: but the honour or glory of kings is to search out a thing" (Prov. 25:2).

Love is worth searching for. It is worth defining, once discovered. There is nothing to compare to it. Love is worth more than all treasures and time. Love is the greatest gift of all. God is Love.

Love seems to be concealed in the world. People try to live without Love and seldom search for it. We want to know someone's status, worth, or possessions rather than whether they are lovable. Heart still matters to a king. A king knows that Love will remain when all else changes.

King Solomon described this fact long ago in the Song of Solomon:

> Many waters cannot quench love, nor will rivers overflow it;
> if a man were to give all the riches of his house for love,
> it would be utterly despised. (Song 8:7)

This Scripture passage was given to me when I was going through a trial in a relationship. The lady was really pressing me about giving her money. I remembered what the Lord had instructed me, and I kept to my convictions. I knew that these needs had nothing to do with me, but were perhaps her reason for seeking a relationship. She told me that I didn't know what Love was, and that our relationship would not work unless I was there for her assistance.

Now, we had only known each other for a couple of weeks. I thought, *Where did all this come from?* My conversation with my heavenly Father stayed in my mind. I realized that God had warned me when I first started this journey of singleness. It seemed this was more than a meeting between a man and a woman. It was a test for my development as a single person.

Then one day I was in prayer at work. I cried out to the Lord about this concern. All of a sudden I heard a voice inside my heart. I knew it was a word of the Lord, saying, "Look up."

Definition of Love

When I looked up, I saw a calendar that my young daughters had given me about three years earlier. It was a Thomas Kinkade desk calendar with a Scripture verse for each day. I had saved it on my birthday and never changed the date. I had never really noticed the verse before that day. It was Song of Solomon 8:7.

Right here, Solomon tells us that money can't buy us Love. This verse is worth memorizing if you are serious about discovering lasting Love. I felt peace deep inside because I knew that heaven had answered my prayers. I was walking in the correct path. I felt that this was a secret Scripture verse, for I had never heard it mentioned. But from that day forward, I knew that what He had spoken to me after my divorce had been confirmed. Sometimes God has ways of making us feel really special. I call this a time of exaltation that comes from remaining humble. He shall lift you up.

True Love Is Unquenchable and Floods Can't Extinguish It.

God is looking at our hearts from the first hello. Hello is big when it comes to Love. Without a good hello, there can be no opportunity for "I do." Few people are prepared to say hello. Yet I have come to recognize that it all begins with hello.

Most people think they have time in a relationship to prepare, change, and develop into who they aren't now. This is not possible; we are who we are when we say hello. Remember the foolish virgins in Matthew 25. I suggest that you read and meditate on the passage.

> Then the kingdom of heaven will be comparable to ten virgins, who took their lamps and went out to meet the bridegroom.
> Five of them were foolish, and five were prudent.
> For when the foolish took their lamps, they took no oil with them,
> but the prudent took oil in flasks along with their lamps. Now while the bridegroom was delaying, they all got drowsy and *began* to sleep.
> But at midnight there was a shout, "Behold, the bridegroom! Come out to meet *him*."
> Then all those virgins rose and trimmed their lamps.

> The foolish said to the prudent, "Give us some of your oil, for our lamps are going out."
> But the prudent answered, "No, there will not be enough for us and you *too*; go instead to the dealers and buy *some* for yourselves."
> And while they were going away to make the purchase, the bridegroom came, and those who were ready went in with him to the wedding feast; and the door was shut. Later the other virgins also came, saying, "Lord, lord, open up for us."
> But he answered, "Truly I say to you, I do not know you."
> Be on the alert then, for you do not know the day nor the hour. (Matt. 25:1–13)

I know we use this parable a lot for teaching about the last days and the coming of the kingdom of heaven. However, I like see it in terms of dealing with singleness and Love. The virgins represent single people. The bridegroom is the answer to their desires and prayers. The story is about being prepared for the answer when the answer is presented. As I mentioned, it all starts at hello.

The bridegroom did come, but some of the virgins were not prepared to say hello. He did not recognize those who were unprepared.

I have learned to always be prepared. No one knows when God will answer the prayer they have prayed. God can answer your prayer at any moment, but unless you are prepared, you may not receive the answer. It can all happen in a flash, like a shout at midnight. I know this very well from my own experiences.

Many have said to me, "You know, I am marriage material." Then they met a real king, and they recognized that what was perhaps good enough for some men wasn't good enough for what they had been praying for. A real Love requires us to be ready.

Love doesn't come to flee or flicker out. Love comes to empower, enrich, enlighten, explore, and explode within and all around us. A hello should be fresh, not stale. When I meet a stale hello, I keep moving. Hello doesn't look back. It looks toward new days, new ways, and new chapters in our lives.

Definition of Love

Here is a good example of what can happen at hello: "The refining pot is for silver and the furnace for gold, But the LORD tests hearts" (Prov. 17:3). This tells me that the time of testing is going to come after the hello. Tests can be as hot as a furnace, but they are necessary. God uses them to purify our hearts and to purify Love by bringing the impurities to the surface. These impurities are in each of us. Seldom do we allow the purifying fires of God to draw them out and His hands to remove them from our lives. I have known this for a long time. However, we are programmed to see disagreements as an ending instead of a beginning.

Remember the fibers of fear I mentioned earlier? There are no shortcuts to a healthy relationship. Each of us will be faced with this impasse. I call it a door, the gateway to Love. Crucial conflicts talked out in crucial conversations will lead us to become united in Love like no other process.

God is at work when we say hello. I believe God tests hearts to let us decide if a relationship is going to endure, grow beyond the door of enchantment, and step into the gateway of Love. Both people in a relationship can grow and go beyond that impasse, which consists of the same things that have stopped each person at the same place in relationship-building time and time again.

Think about this. We were just a step away from entering an environment of Love that we may never need to experience or discover again.

When the fear, the pain, and the burn that arise are allowed to shape our hearts, we are seldom able to be our true selves with one another. Fear will always repel, reject, and resist Love. God knows that it takes heat to put a true couple together for a lasting Love. When there is a divorce, it takes similar heat to pull the couple apart and make them into individuals again.

One thing a couple can count on is that the test is coming. God doesn't let us into His plan, but He tells us that He will test our hearts. We have all heard that Love can stand up to the test of time. As believers, we should know this. Love will be tested, and a true Love will stand any test. God so loved and He is still Love and loving today. When the test comes, if two people are ready for Love, they can use it to improve their relationship and make it stronger. But both parties have to work and be willing to get involved in the purification process.

Why Are People Afraid of Love?

Remember this and never forget it: lasting Love requires work. Many people are seeking a relationship, but they forget the work that it will require. A relationship isn't a want but lots of work.

As a former metallurgist and material scientist, I know that getting metals to the purest stages of processing takes intense heat. Lots of fire is required to get materials to their boiling points. Then the impurities will surface and can be removed. A few impurities will remain; there is no such thing as a perfect Love matches. Nevertheless, there is Love made by working together and occasionally removing the remaining impurities.

This is what God wants to do for us—purify our hearts so that those few impurities will not hinder the Love process and growth in our relationships. Love needs fire, and these fires will bring the desire to work on what is needed to develop into something special and lasting. We can call this the passion in Love making, not in a bedroom but in our hearts.

When we are afraid of Love, we can never have the full fires of passion. Lust's passion is fading and powerless. But Love's passion is a fire that is everlasting and full of creative power. Love's passion energizes anyone to do the works of Love that are required to keep a healthy and lasting relationship alive. Perhaps fear is simply the fuel that is needed to ignite a flame of Love that gets hotter each time we push beyond where we have been. We can use fear by casting it out or leaving it outside when we step through the door of perfect Love.

Love requires testing.

Again a reminder that King Solomon knew this long ago:

> Put me like a seal over your heart,
> Like a seal on your arm.
> For love is as *strong as death*,
> Jealousy is as severe as Sheol;
> Its flashes are flashes of fire,
> The *very* flame of the LORD.
> Many waters cannot quench love,
> Nor will rivers overflow it;
> If a man were to give all the riches of his house for love,
> It would be utterly despised." (Song 8:6–7, my emphasis)

Definition of Love

We see here that Love is as strong as death and no water can quench it. Love is defined as hot and is called the flame of God. God will test the hearts of lovers. To melt and mold hearts into one, He uses the very things that fear causes us to avoid.

We need to know that the days and times of enchantment will leave us. Enchantment Love is always fleeing, never settled. It searches for a way out. Each person must realize, "This is someone I want to be with. I can't be without them, nor can they be without me." This is when we have to make the decision to walk through the gateway of Love or break up and move on. Break up will usually occur when a couple does not desire to walk through the door of conflict into the room of a deeper relationship where Love is directing each to go.

We have all faced these doors before in every relationship that we have been in. We stay on the other side of the gateway, not wanting to rock the boat or step into a more serious stage of the relationship. I call this the surface-dwelling or enchantment stage. We just want to have fun, nothing serious. But in our hearts, we want to get beyond where we have been.

The time of enchantment will erode. The phone calls, text messages, Facebook postings, late-night conversations, and planning will come to a slow stop. Each person's eyes will be opened to the other's shortcomings. These will become more than a background shadow; they will become front and center. Instead of having a real talk to step beyond this impasse, we will avoid and shrink back. Love begins to fade. Fear surfaces, this time with a grip of death.

Fear has placed us all in that situation at one time or another. Many of you can relate to this process of how the test comes to purify our hearts for Love. Perhaps you met the right person, but neither of you had the tools, skills, or abilities to push beyond this impasse into a world of Love that does exist.

Love will be tested, and it will be tested by God. God is into creating what is good and perfect. This impasse in relationships is real. God places it there to enable the couple to work, cultivate faithfulness, and keep alive the Love that He has given to each for the other.

The Bible says that faith without works is dead and that faith works by Love. Another definition of Love from the Song of Solomon is that

Why Are People Afraid of Love?

Love is stronger than death. Love will keep our faith working and make all mountains move. Nothing shall stand before us. If God is for us, who or what can be against us?

Love will fight and overcome, when it is real Love. *Love can be defined as the ability to remain together when difficult times come.* Nothing can separate us from the Love of God or our Love for one another. Love isn't easily destroyed or removed. It is strong. It is a bond that isn't easily broken.

This Love isn't imaginary. It isn't found only in a good book or chick flick. It is not for everyone. It is for those who have put their trust in God and believe in one another to do what is necessary to stay together.

> For this reason I bow my knees before the Father,
> from whom every family in heaven and on earth derives its name,
> that He would grant you, according to the riches of His glory, to be strengthened with power through His Spirit in the inner man,
> so that Christ may dwell in your hearts through faith; *and that you, being rooted and grounded in love,*
> may be able to comprehend with all the saints what is the breadth and length and height and depth,
> and to know the love of Christ which surpasses knowledge, that you may be filled up to all the fullness of God.
> Now to Him who is able to do far more abundantly beyond all that we ask or think, according to the power that works within us,
> to Him *be* the glory in the church and in Christ Jesus to all generations forever and ever. Amen. (Eph. 3:14–21, my emphasis)

This is all a work of faith. We need to define Love before we can go out searching for it or welcome it into our hearts. Faith dwelling in our hearts will keep us rooted and grounded in Love. To me that mean, we stop plucking up our roots and moving on each time a conflict arises. Instead, we learn how to work on things together. When someone isn't ready or willing to work on a true conflict, then you know that person isn't prepared to go beyond the times of enchantment. That person isn't ready to walk through that door of infinite possibilities of Love.

Apostle Paul called being rooted in Love the depth, breadth, length, or height of knowing the Love of Christ, which surpasses all knowledge. I believe it is the same for us all. Fear desires to keep us from ever experiencing this rooted and grounded Love that last and grows continuously. When something is rooted, that means it has broken through the surface and gotten some staying power to stand the storms of testing. This process of working is not normally seen by others, for it is below the surface. When it breaks through, everyone witnesses the fruit of Love in our lives.

You have to define Love and know what it is for yourself. If you know what Love is, then you can determine what Love isn't. Love isn't something light and fake. It is stronger than death and hotter than a flame. No flood can quench it. It can cause us to be rooted and grounded. When the season of testing is over, the fear of hurt will be removed and replaced by the knowledge of Love. This knowledge will enable us to comprehend the breadth and length and height and depth of the Love that God intends for us. That Love, which is the only Love, is good, perfect, and lasting. It comes from above, and He adds no sorrow to it.

I have often heard people say what they aren't looking for when it comes to a relationship. This normally tells me the kind of relationships they have encountered. They have their force shields up and their inspection scopes out to make sure that they don't encounter again what they aren't looking for. Remember that fear attracts more fears. Scripture says, "For what I fear comes upon me, And what I dread befalls me" (Job 3:25).

Fear knows what it is doing; it is here to keep us from finding Love. When I hear rejections spoken, I know that person will likely not experience Love until they begin the process of removing this fear from their hearts. They must begin to speak words of faith. Faith is hope, and the evidence will follow.

We've got to learn to hear what is coming out of our hearts and souls and act accordingly. Some people refuse to hear. They keep attracting fear to their environment of fear. Family and friends may agree with us because they too have never been rooted and grounded in Love. Just one word of fear can paralyze the hope for a promising relationship.

Job said, "For my groaning comes at the sight of my food, And my cries pour out like water" (Job 3:24). The thoughts and words within our hearts can become groaning, which will eventually pour out from our lips.

I say again, no one is perfect. I have a saying: "If you are afraid of the hurt, don't start the search." We all want someone in our lives. But can we see why things don't go much further than before? We start again with a different face, but it takes us to the same place. Perhaps the concern isn't with those we meet but with our own hearts and souls.

God tests hearts. He reveals that this time of singleness is a time for each of us to learn about Love and discover its true meaning. Trial and error are a part of life. Trying to live life mistake-free is not living but another form of fear operating in control. This unmasked fear will sooner or later will become no life at all, just plain wasted years. Do you agree that a dead person can make no more mistakes?

The uncertainty of what things will become is just part of the path of singleness. If you want to discover Love, you have to begin to seek it within your own heart. Why are we afraid when we really want to love and be loved? I think it all begins with defining Love. Once we know what it is, we can discover it within another's soul.

Then we will know that the life lessons we have had have worked. We will be rooted and grounded because of experience that words can no longer express—Love.

The definition of Love can lessen or even remove fear. New fears may arise, but the same approach of growing will enable one to move past the fear every time. Keep this simple definition of Love in mind that I mentioned in chapter 4: **"Love is simply a mutual agreement between two individuals to be committed to one another. When everything else changes, Love will remain because of their commitment."**

For many years, I held that verse from the Song of Solomon in my heart. I placed it in this manuscript in 2012. Finally, I heard it used in the wedding ceremony of Prince Harry and Megan Markle, on May 19, 2018. To me, it was a testimony and confirmation of this book and of the season to share it with the world. A door had been opened for the entire world to hear and be reminded of what Love is.

Love Lessons from Chapter 5

Why not take the time to do some self-talk? Listen to your own words and thoughts when meeting someone for the first time. Using the page below for your reflections, date and then feel the source from which those thoughts have come. Is it fear or is it Love? If it is fear, then continue to write down what the thoughts of Love would be. How would Love's thoughts change your daily outlook on relationship-building? Write down your definition of Love and think of how it may guide you in the future. Write down the definition of Love that you derive from God's Word each time you read it.

Prayer

Lord, I pray for your Spirit of Grace to be poured out to open hearts. Help us to walk through the storms of life and through the open door of Your presence, promises, and purposes. May we begin to submit to You our Love lives, and to resist the fear from the past. May we all experience the true definition of Love that is given by You for each of us to share with another.
In Jesus's name,
Amen

THE POWER OF LOVE

Rockets have lifted off
Bombs have burst
Space missions have been accomplished
To escape the atmosphere of the earth

Atomic age has created
Weapons to settle conflicts
While hearts seem to be yearning
For Love to fill them

No amount of money
No measurement of time
Can give anyone
What true Love defines.

Saying goodbye to one's fears
Learning the lessons of Love
Can help get one ready and set
For a real-time explosion

Heart to heart
Mind to mind
Eye to eye
Who cares about the time?

The time it takes
To discover one another
Glad it didn't take forever
For either of us to see

Kaboom! We are still here!
Even after Love has been ignited
What an explosion!
Share between us

He is the Giver
He enables us to find
What our hearts yearn for
His eternal gift of Love

What a power
Didn't take a lifetime to harness
Once it is within our hearts
It creates the energy to know

No matter what difficulties
That may cross our paths
The power of Love
Will enable us to pass

Listen to Love
Peace will surround
Where confusion once existed
Now soundness abounds

The power of Love
Removes all fears
Now we can unite
And begin to really live

You and me
Let our eyes see
U-S, U-S, U-S

For now on in everything
The power that Love brings
In you and in me

Priceless Production

REFLECTIONS FOR CHAPTER 5

Take a few moments and think about how you many have defined love in your life? Write down how you can begin to adapt the definitions of love in your love life going forward.

Loving someone is the best investment ever made.

—Apostle Tony K. Thomas

CHAPTER 6
Love Has to Be Given

When I was given this assignment, I thought that it was much too difficult and a bit embarrassing. It still is unnerving even several years after God commissioned me. I am slow in a lot of ways, mainly in completely obeying God, because I prefer God to use someone else. I like taking the backseat approach to life and leading from behind the scenes. I am an intercessor of sorts, willing to pray the mission through but use someone else to implement it. I find it easy to share God's Word on many topics as the Spirit provides the demonstration of His presence and power.

However, I am what I would call the least qualified to speak about Love. So many of my attempts resulted in the same outcome—another failed relationship. I know that God chooses the weak and foolish to give strength and wisdom. This way He knows that the vessel must depend on Him to pour in as He pours out.

I do see the importance of this great subject, especially in the times that are upon us. Remember what Jesus said: "Because lawlessness is increased, most people's love will grow cold" (Matt. 24:12).

I asked God several times why I was given this assignment. He revealed that He knew I would pay attention to the details in this journey of singleness. I had never thought that I would have experiences that meant something later. However, I do believe that the steps of a good man are ordained by the Lord. Though that man may stumble, he will not fall or remain down.

> The steps of a man are established by the LORD,
> And He delights in his way.
> When he falls, he will not be hurled headlong
> Because the LORD is the One who holds his hand. (Ps. 37:23–24)

This is a very profound passage, because it tells of God's protective system, which I call GPS. God is truly with those who are with Him. Years later, I still notice His hand holding me up and leading me forward by the insight and wisdom from His Spirit. He let me know that this singleness journey has a purpose, not only for my life but for the lives of others.

When I first became born again, the Spirit revealed to me, "The life that you now live, you will no longer live it for yourself but for others." It is important to give your life to Christ early in life, and witness what can become of it through the years. Today, I see His hand did hold my hands, even in guiding them to write these books. His kingdom has come and His will is being done. This isn't just a work for singles but for all who desire to harvest Love in their lives.

Let's go back to Proverbs 31. Verse 10 was where I normally started when I read this chapter prior to that 2004 New Year's morning.

> A capable, intelligent, and virtuous woman—who can find her?
> She is far more precious than jewels and her value is far above rubies or pearls. (Prov. 31:10 AMP)

I had never noticed the question mark before. At the moment that I was rereading this, led by the Spirit, that question mark looked as big as the Empire State Building in my mind and heart. This was a big discovery. It took the pressure off of me in searching for a mate.

I realized in that very moment that I had been searching on my own, and that wasn't His intent. God wants us to know that our search begin with Him and ends with Him presenting that perfect gift of Love to each of us.

Remember, a king will search a thing out. We've just got to give our prayers a little time to reset and refresh our spirits, souls, and minds. God saying, "Who can find?" The question turns our efforts from our own works to trusting in our heavenly Father. Trusting God works every time.

We Can't Find Love on Our Own

The biggest reason that people are afraid of Love is because their hope to discover Love is based on their works and not on the works of God. We have to seek God first and foremost to be able to find true Love. It isn't lost, but we are lost in our methods and pursuit of it.

It is important to have and know the true definition of Love. Love is defined by God's Word and His works in our lives. Knowing what Love is can keep one from unnecessary stress and emotional turmoil.

Finding Love is like trying to find a treasure. We can't find Love on our own without first asking, seeking, and knocking for guidance from our heavenly Father. Love does exist. It isn't lost, nor is it outside of our reach. Love is discovered with God's help.

The Word of God possesses *true keys* in the discovery of Love. The most important is revealing what Love is not. The word *love* has many definitions, according to the ancient Greeks. Some of these are *agape* (love of God or love for everyone), *eros* (sexual passion), *philia* (a deep friendship), *pliautia* (self-love), *storge* (parental affection), *ludus* (playful love, flirting), and *pragma* (mature understanding of love). Each Greek term for Love is a component in what makes up a total Love, which can exist in every relationship in life. Reviewing each of these definitions or components of Love is beneficial in helping one grasp the depth and importance of Love in one's life. Also, this is a reminder of how ancient the subject of defining Love is.

As I said before, this assignment isn't easy. It takes complete openness to be used by God's Spirit to share with His body. My desire is that many will read this—not to seek to be entertained, but to be instructed in their pursuit of Love and the removal of their biggest obstacle to Love, which is fear.

I have had to walk away from this writing for months, even a year at a time, just to get comfortable with all that I desire to reveal. I am still unable to reveal all that the Spirit desires me to share. However, I hope that this writing will open up to you a scriptural context that you may not have been aware of before.

I want to let you know this fact: *God is not afraid of Love.* God wants to instruct us in every area of our lives. His desire for you and me is to give us His best, and His best is a good and perfect gift that comes from above. I believe that for many people, that gift is the blessing of lasting Love in their lives.

Look at one of the most quoted passages in the Bible: "God so loved the world that he gave his only begotten son" (John 3:16). This passage gives us a glimpse into the mind-set and heart of God. We see that He loved even before we were created or gave Him our respect. Many times God has used this passage to pull me out of the path of fear and let me know that what I was experiencing were just growing pains.

Sometimes it may seem you are being taken advantage of or even used. Well, think about the Love of God. He keeps giving to the entire world every single day for all eternity. He loved before any of us ever said that we loved Him or asked Him into our hearts as Lord and Savior.

Often when I lift up those kinds of thoughts to heaven, I realize that I was really having another selfish moment. Then I repent or apologize and give thanks that I am learning and developing to get beyond this point. I realize that I am being taught by the Holy Spirit, just as He promised, to teach and define for me what Love is based upon His Word.

I had to learn that I must grow and go on even if someone I am with is still struggling with the speck of fear within their soul. It isn't hard to recognize this fear in another, once you begin your new journey led by the Love of God. Frustrations will set in—but only for a moment before you have to release them to heaven and see the bigger picture. Without a doubt, there is no one who has ever loved like Father, Son, and Holy Spirit has.

I recall a picture that I once saw of the cross. Inside it were these words: "I asked the Lord how much did He love me, and He stretched out His arms and uttered, 'It is finished' and died." Each time I get my mind back to the finished works of Calvary, I know that I can forgive and give more. What I gave was more for my benefit in the search to discover the Love of my life.

This is what I call "minute by minute miracle-working power" (M^3P). It is a miracle to be able to let go and grow. We begin to learn not to fall in Love but to grow in Love. If we fall in Love, we will in time fall out of Love. When we grow in Love, we will become more loving and lovable over time.

This is similar to our spiritual growth in Christ. Scripture says that we are to grow in the grace and knowledge of our Lord and Savior. We don't begin our Christian journey knowing all about God. We learn to love Him more as we experience His great Love for us in our daily lives.

Jesus told us to pick up our crosses and follow Him. We must learn to die daily. Love is about giving, and to give, one must not put oneself first, but another. This is how we learn that Love isn't based on what is received. *Love has to be given.*

One of the reasons that we are afraid of Love is because we don't think that we will receive it from the people we give it to. When we are afraid of Love, we seldom give it with our whole hearts. Love has to be given without any notion of reward. You can't put conditions on it, such as, "I will say I love you after I hear you say that you love me." I have witnessed this over and over personally. I have heard ladies say that it isn't a woman's place to say "I love you" first. I am still searching for where that information came from.

This isn't Love. This is what those who are *afraid* of Love do. Very few people in this frame of mind will experience true Love. Nevertheless, Love is given to all by God.

The gospel of Luke reads, "Treat others the same way you want them to treat you. If you love those who love you, what credit is *that* to you? For even sinners love those who love them" (Luke 6:31–32). This admonition should be taken into account when we are learning about Love. In the Beatitudes, Jesus's subject was Love. Scripture even mentions loving the unlovable in one's life. If we are told to love our enemies, how much more should we love other people we are getting to know?

Worldly ways have become the norm for loving. Today, we can witness the Love of many has become cold or even waxed upon their stony hearts. Jesus knows that God has given each of us the power to Love. We have the power to give Love to another. Love isn't something that we toy with or try to command and direct. Likewise, Love isn't something that we go out to possess or conquer, like it's some trophy we hoist. Love is free and should be given freely. We only possess it when we become it, by giving and being more loving. When Love is given with the expectation of reward, it did not originate with God, but from within our own souls. When we can only feel, speak, or give Love after we receive it, then we are no better than those who do not know Love.

This is a very powerful concept, especially in today's world of lovelessness. Love is the greatest investment known to humankind. We have to give it in order to see a return. Once we give it, we have to let go of it and let the dividends of time do their work to help Love grow into something more rewarding than our initial investment.

Fear is the only reason why many never make that initial investment of Love. "What the wicked fears will come upon him, but the desire of the righteous will be granted" (Prov. 10:24). God sees things differently from the way we see things. He calls the wicked those who are led by their fears.

It takes the same effort to walk in Love as it does to walk in fear. If we desire Love, we will be granted Love. This isn't something that we just do; it is something that we learn to do by recognizing our previous setbacks and realizing that we need help. We know that only God can find and define Love for us. That is what Proverbs 31:10 means: "Who can find?"

Why are we afraid to be first to say "I love you" and leave it alone? Why can't we keep saying it without any expectations? I believe that when we learn this principle, we will discover the unending reward of loving and being loved. *God is Love*! God is still the Giver of Love to all who walk in His Love. His Love has no fear or hesitation. "Give, and it will be given to you. They will pour into your lap a good measure—pressed down, shaken together, *and* running over. For by your standard of measure it will be measured to you in return" (Luke 6:38).

These are words from Christ our Savior. These are not from the latest TV show or from today's vernacular. Jesus spoke these words, and they still are relevant today. These words can be used with almost anything we do for another person. The more you give, the more will be returned.

I call this a true investment with a perfect return. You know that it will come back to you. It may not come back from the person you are with now, but it will be returned, and not in the same measure but overflowing.

Love Has to Be Given

Sometimes the thoughts of the world may creep into my mind when it comes to doing something sweet and precious for another person. That is when you need to push past the fear and just do it. I know there is something greater in this moment of giving that is beyond what I can see. This is not a "give to get," but giving because it is right and proper. It is all within your power; you set the standard by which you decide to give.

Some people have become used to giving very little when getting to know another person. Most people do not even know this biblical principle, and this is why so many of their past relationships were not successful. They expect to receive the best while giving their least. We all need to know that heaven is watching each of us.

Fear is our source of rewards when we operate under its control. Fear keeps us from giving our best every time. Fear provides no return. Think about that for a moment. Love's return is in knowing that in due season, you shall reap. That reaping comes from the Father of Lights. Our Father gives every good and perfect gift from above.

We are not from the world; we are from God. We should not love like the world, giving to get or getting before we give. Love has to be given. Apostle John gave us these words as our example to follow when it comes to Love:

> You are from God, little children, and have overcome them; because greater is He who is in you than he who is in the world.
> They are from the world; therefore they speak *as* from the world, and the world listens to them…
> Beloved, let us love one another, for love is from God; and everyone who loves is born of God and knows God. The one who does not love does not know God, for God is love.
> (1 John 4:5, 7–8)

God has placed in each of us the power of Love. We can overcome all fear because of the greater One within our souls. Jesus is Love, and Love overcomes the ways of the world. This isn't easy by any means, since most people—Christians as well as non-Christians—have adopted the ideology of worldly love, which the Greeks termed *eros*. This is a sign of the times and a signal for the return of Christ.

We who are in Christ must decide to keep loving and giving Love, no matter what happens. A new excitement should arise within your soul, knowing that you will be blessed by giving Love.

We can never out give God, nor can we ever exhaust the power of Love. We must learn to practice and proclaim our Love as we desire to be loved. God is the Source that gave. He has put Love in our hearts, not necessarily for ourselves but for others. I believe if we give what has been given, we will in turn receive it back in much greater measure, as Scripture says. *Love has to be given.* Remember that, and I believe it will be abundantly returned.

The Greek word *agape* was left in their dictionary for many centuries because there was no one who could possess such Love. It wasn't until the writing of the New Testament that *agape* was placed in Scripture as the God kind of Love. God's Love isn't measured by the deeds of mankind. It is the same throughout all the ages. God is Love and Love is God. With Christ in our hearts, we are now possessors of *agape*.

Love Lessons from Chapter 6

Take a moment to pray and ask the Holy Spirit to bring back to you the times when you withheld Love or didn't verbalize Love in your relationship-building because you were afraid that the other person might not love you back. Write down how you would have felt if you had just given Love and left it alone. Use the page of reflections for chapter 6 to write down your thoughts.

Prayer

Oh Father of light, life, and Love, may you shine a ray of hope into the soul of the readers and let each know that your Love has never lost its power.

In Jesus's name,
Amen

Love is our best investment

REFLECTIONS FOR CHAPTER 6

Fear freezes us up while Love thaws us out.

—Apostle Tony K. Thomas

CHAPTER 7

Love Is an Action, Not just a Feeling

Love is an action, not just words or feelings. Love moved God to give, but not to give just anything. God gave the world His very best. There is still no substitute for what God has given—His only Son.

Some people give a little and expect to receive everything in return. This brings to mind one of my encounters. A lady whom I was dating mentioned her thoughts about giving and sharing in a relationship. Her opinion was that it should be 80 percent giving by her man to her giving only 20 percent.

I said that Love isn't an insurance policy or ground beef. It doesn't seek its own or move in selfishness. Love is giving, and that requires 100 percent from all of us. It's 100 percent to 100 percent.

Her fears were entangled in her statement. She was seeking another's 100 percent to her own 20 percent. The whole time that we dated, the relationship was out of balance. Love is more than a word; it's in everything we do, say, and give.

God didn't wait to see what the world would give in return for His Love. God so loved that He gave. He didn't have to give it again. God knew that not every human being in the world from eternity would desire His Love. However, He still gave. Those who will receive it and believe it will obtain the benefit—*eternal life*.

This is why we need to possess *agape*, the God kind of Love. We need *agape* not just in a spiritual sense, but in our lives. We need it that much more in our Love lives, to sustain lasting and healthy relationships. We can give Love unconditionally and do it with joy.

When we are free to love, I believe that Love will be discovered. Until that time, we need to embrace the Love that is allowed to come into our lives as an experience to remove our fear. Then we can discover what is inside our hearts, which no one else may ever know.

So often we walk or live in a way that is contrary to what we want. We ask God for one thing but settle for something else. We sometimes believe that there is no perfect Love for us.

However, Love is here to help and assist in our growing into a more loving and lovable person. It isn't our slave or doormat. *Love is a powerful force.* It is not to be played with or taken lightly, if we want to receive the wonders of its gifts. Love keeps giving no matter what another does with it.

WHEN LOVE DOESN'T CARE

So often we get stuck behind
Things that really don't matter
We focus on the what-ifs
And let the choice become rather

We seem not to get past
The speck in our eyes
Soon we forget about the times
Special moments and spices in life

Where did the Love go?
Where did it hide?
Where is the sweetness?
Why did it sour?

Once the words become few
The feelings begin to dissipate
The emotions return
To that safe ol' place

When we really think about it
What does Love care
About things that surround us
When Love isn't there?

Love doesn't care about the specks
When you are there to enjoy
Love doesn't care for the troubles
When we have each other to rejoice

Why Are People Afraid of Love?

> Love should be our focus
> Not anything else
> More than a word that is spoken
> When Love appears
> Love simply doesn't care
>
> Priceless Production

The poem that I shared earlier, "The Force of Love," is one I wrote many years ago at twenty years of age. Let me tell you, I knew very little about Love at that time. Therefore, I know that those words were inspired by a Divine Power. The poem spoke the truth. More than three decades later, I wrote the above poem. It speaks more profoundly about perfect Love. This Love will remain after all else dissipates. Nothing can scare this Love, no amount of hurts or disappointments. What does Love care about what we have been through or are going to go through?

The difficulty is that so many people's fears about Love come from their not-so-good experiences. We have tattooed each negative experience into our memory banks. We have made the declarations "Never again!" so many times. We need to perform a total auto-erase on these memories and upload new experience that comes from learning what Love is. God is able to forgive and forget our sins once we are able to truly confess and repent. Repentance isn't a constant mental battle of self-affliction but simply a change of heart, mind or ways. We should never have to mention them again or fear that God will hold them against us. We simply learn, grow and go beyond by practicing loving more.

God is merciful. We are told to be merciful, but are we willing to let go and let God? I give God praise for His mercy and loving-kindness toward us. God takes our sins and casts them into the sea of forgetfulness. He isn't able to recall them even if He wanted to. We have to learn to do the same with our past failed relationships. We keep these past experiences fresh and alive each time we speak about things like how long we've been divorced, how long we've been single, and how we feel about our disappointments. We've got to let them go so we can grow. I hope you hear what I am saying. We've got to erase these past painful memories from our lives. We can eliminate the sting of these experiences and yet allow their benefits to exist by burying the past pain. Perhaps, if we are honest with ourselves, we can recognize that we contributed to that pain. We can bring forward things that can help us to make better decisions in knowing that fear has no benefit.

I am no expert in "auto-erasing." I have discovered the results of not letting past pain and failures go. Failure to let go will only bring more of the same. So today, I reflect upon the gains and pleasure and not the pain and sorrow. Without these experiences, we would never get involved or have the opportunity to discover Love. So what if a relationship didn't work? The benefit is that we were able to love and be loved again.

I know about this firsthand. That is perhaps the reason this book is being written. I needed help and asked of God and He did. I think that He got tired of hearing me pray that same ol' weary prayers about Love and relationships. I remember that time as if it were a few minutes ago. I am sure that you have had your share of offering up these kinds of prayers if you are single and serious about finding the Love of your life.

There are times when we can look back. But we don't look back to fill our hearts with more pain and fear. We look back with the freedom of seeing the mighty hand of God at work in the situation. I can recall that God had to step into a relationship that I was about to move into in a serious way toward marriage. I was very much in love, but I did recognize that there were major issues that needed to be addressed. We went to counseling. But I later determined that I needed to let this lady go and move on.

I was in a really low place at that time. But I recognized that I had made the right decision and was guided by the Father above. I remember a time of prayer. I was speaking to God about this relationship. I thought that God would reconnect us and correct the issues. The Spirit of God spoke to me from within my heart, asking me if I was hurt. My reply was yes. I was hurt—very much so. I had been single for several years, and I was ready for that part of my life to be over. I wanted to begin a new chapter. The Spirit of God spoke again and asked me if I loved this lady. I immediately replied yes, I loved her with all my heart. Then I received this message from the Holy Spirit: "At least you know that you can still love."

My thoughts were no longer about the failure or the hurt, but about knowing that I was on my way to recovery and the healing of my heart. Pains and disappointments can be buried. New opportunities would arise. This was the beginning of my heart thawing by the power of Love.

So I ask you again—so what if a relationship doesn't work? I believe that when you decide to love and allow the Love to be given without control or fear, it will benefit you no matter what happens. Love is our best teaching, it requires each of us to give Love and leave the results to our heavenly Father who is Love.

Continue to Love until You Find the Love of a Lifetime

Love isn't lost, but it isn't where most of us are seeking it. Remember, who can find? Practice, practice, practice is what we need. We've got to make a conscious effort to rise above the disappointments and setbacks. We do this by accepting God's plan and implementing it into our lives. Practice doesn't make things perfect, but it sure can make things better.

Say this again, and feel the flow of possibilities: *practice doesn't make things perfect, but it sure can make things better.*

Even at times when it seems like nothing is working; just know it *is* working, because you are allowing it to work in your life.

It is easy to read a book or listen to a so-called expert on the subject of Love. But I find that few invest in becoming educated about Love. I had to enroll in what I call Love school, taught by none other than our heavenly Father, who is Love. We continue to talk with people who live in their past pains, and we seldom rise above our own. Remember that *we have a future if we want one.*

On that day when I was thinking that the Lord would restore my failed and un-healthy relationship. I realized that I wanted the relationship not for permanency, but for the healing of my heart. I wanted to end singleness. You have to stay in the game of singleness until the perfect and lasing Love is returned back to you. I believe this will come about by gaining the skills, tools, and abilities that come from loving the way that Love requires. Once we gain these tools, we need to practice with them and develop the ability to use our knowledge of loving, no matter what. Again, practice doesn't make things perfect—just better.

There are many tools we need to learn to use to be able to auto-erase our past. You've got to want to do this. You've got to let it go. Many people are more in love with their pasts than with their future freedom. I hear things like "You just don't understand my situation" or "I don't want to be hurt again" or "I am tired of the games people play." I witness this often: blaming others instead of accepting one's own part in the matter. Blaming others is a great indicator that one isn't ready to move forward. Auto-erasing is the only way to get beyond where you are. Auto-erasing is the time when you simply choose to forget and move on.

Auto-erase will remove the blame. It will allow you to accept the changes and gain the knowledge that only Love can bring.

You need to write this down and put it in daily view. Never forget these words: *remove the blame* and accept the changes for a future Love in your life.

It is no one's fault that we fail in our pursuit of Love. But it can be our fault if we never learn or gain the skills, abilities, and tools for developing a lasting Love. Fear will always be, but perfect Love will always overcome fear. We all have fear, but it is much different when you know that fear has no benefits for you. Fear has frozen many in their attempt at loving, but when Love is allowed to do its work, our hearts will thaw and flow again with hope and joy.

Many are afraid of Love because it isn't visible. It can't be seen, touched, or tasted. Love is more than an emotion. Love is far more than temporary pleasures or fulfillment. *Love is essentially everything.*

The tools and skills of Love are available to learn and to use in our search to find and eventually keep Love in our lives. I believe the first place we need to look isn't the latest online site that offers up the flesh and fear in a package for what seems like a small price. We need to start our search by *seeking the Word of God*.

The Spirit of God is waiting for us to give Him permission to guide us into all truths. Remember the words of Christ: "The Truth will set you free." This freedom is powerful for those who desire a true and lasting Love.

Remember Proverbs 31, the verse about who can find? The question mark is there for those who will discover that they can't do this on their own, only with the help of the Spirit of the Lord. We need to say, "*Help!*" Help is a big step in the right direction. I think it is the open door. Before we ask for help, we are most likely working things out in our own ways. Asking for help lets God know that we are ready for His assistance.

The tool of auto-erase enables us to give ourselves and others a chance at Love. Once you discover this tool, don't be surprised by the fear it creates in others. They will realize that you are free and that you are truly seeking God's best for yourself.

The verse from the Love chapter in the Bible says it best. I believe this is the way to auto-erase. We have to grow up in Love, to the point that we know it is worth our future to stop keeping a record of all the wrongs we've suffered. Forgiveness is a verb or action, not a feeling. It is something we must do, not just ignore or pray for. It must be done to understand the benefits of Love. Remember, Love is an action not just a feeling.

> Love is patient, love is kind *and* is not jealous; love does not brag *and* is not arrogant,
> does not act unbecomingly; it does not seek its own, is not provoked, *does not take into account a wrong suffered*,
> does not rejoice in unrighteousness, but rejoices with the truth;
> bears all things, believes all things, hopes all things, endures all things.
> Love never fails. (1 Cor. 13:4–8, my emphasis)

I have found that people are not use to honesty, kindness, and respect in today's world of singleness, and perhaps not even in marriage. Fear has shaped our world not to believe in the human spirit of honesty and trust. We hear people say, "I don't trust anyone farther than I can see them."

> For what I fear comes upon me, And what I dread befalls me.
> I am not at ease, nor am I quiet, And I am not at rest, but turmoil comes. (Job 3:25–26)

I have discovered many people are so tormented by their fear that their minds manufacture more of it, and it becomes very real to them. If this is you and you realize it, ask God's Spirit for help.

Fear has never produced any kind of Love. Fear is what we are used to until we can see God's ways are beyond our own. His Word will speak to our hearts if we are willing to bring our hearts to Him. Fear can blind us so much that we think we are in Love when we are nowhere near Love. Fear will tell us not to be the first to say "I love you" or "Don't give too much too soon."

We all have experienced these thoughts. Have they ever been true? Have they ever been beneficial in getting to know someone? Job said that he could not find rest, ease, or quiet because of his fears. I believe this is what goes on in one's soul when one is possessed by the fear of loving again.

As I mentioned previously, my every thought and prayer was for a mate, but I couldn't even say the word *wife* in my prayers. That, my friend, is no rest or quiet. Our souls will let us know where we are when it comes to overcoming fear. The turmoil is one broken relationship after another one. For myself, I can now say that is the past. Once you can recognize this pattern in seeking Love, ask for help. A simple prayer is all that is needed, but it has to be real. All these setbacks have hedged you in. See that great light and open door leading to freedom from fear and opportunity for Love.

Love speaks and rejoices with the truth. The Bible tells us to speak the truth in Love. Love will speak your desires and your thoughts. Share, give, and reveal, because Love is seeking to discover, not be covered.

Love will seek the highest interest of another. Jesus said for us to let our light shine. It is good to share some of the experiences that have assisted you in developing your victory over fear. We all have our own war stories. We didn't let them stop us. I hope our experiences enhanced us to know that God is still guiding us to our destination. Past experiences should bring us to a point in our lives where we desire a change. I am speaking to those who are at that point and are ready to move beyond their past pain into the power to attract Love into their lives.

Read aloud the following Scripture passage:

"Why is light given to a man whose way is hidden, And whom God has hedged in?" (Job 3:23).

Could the Spirit of God have led you to this stage in your search for Love? Are you ready to cry for help? Only you know the depth of your

Why Are People Afraid of Love?

search and the longing of your heart. Only you know how many times you have done the same ol' things and expecting a different outcome. I believe this passage from Job is a good word for this point, when it seems that the way to discovering Love is hidden and there is no way beyond where we are in relationship-building. Our God is supreme. He knows where you are. He knew the day would come when you would feel no way out. He knew you would lift up your head in supplication to heaven.

Immediately, the light comes on and the open door is seen. God's purpose is that door. You can once again see God's purpose for you in being single, and how to remove the log of fear from your spiritual eyes. We are all familiar with these words from the Psalmist: "Your word is a lamp to my feet, And a light to my path" (Ps. 119:105). The Word of God is the light that He uses for our GPS. When that light appears, it is there to lead you beyond and into His purposes.

Being afraid of Love isn't in any way normal. It is a serious, learned behavior. As humans, we naturally stay away from things that bring us pain, even emotional pain. We all have heard people say, "I am protecting my heart." But I find these same folk always fall for the very things that they are trying to avoid.

Why is this so? Perhaps they have never gained the knowledge of how to attract Love. Love is not just another fun time to escape past pain. Love requires us to work on ourselves to be prepared for another. Love will move us beyond all our fear and past pain. I want to say this again: God is Love. God created us in His image and in His likeness. Therefore, God didn't give us the spirit of fear. "For God *has not given us a spirit of timidity, but of power and love and discipline*" (2 Tim. 1:7, my emphasis). In the Amplified Classic Version, this same verse reads, "For God did not give us a spirit of timidity *or* cowardice *or* fear, but [He has given us a spirit] of power and of love and of sound judgment *and* personal discipline [abilities that result in a calm, well-balanced mind and self-control]."

Let this passage soak into your soul. I have meditated on this passage many times. This is a powerful key to walking in the principles of God's kingdom.

Where did this fear come from? We learn here that it doesn't come from God. The things that come from God are power, Love, and peace of mind. This tells me that auto-erasing our past pain and sorrow is for

Love Is an Action, Not just a Feeling

our best. We all have a past, especially if you are divorced or have been single for long time. However, let your past be the reason to move on. Don't remain in its pain. Don't become trapped by the fear of yesteryear. Simply forgive and allow the Spirit of God to assist you in the removal of the final fragments of pain.

Being afraid to Love will cause us to surrender the power, Love, and soundness in our lives. There is power when Love is discovered; you will know that it is a powerful way to live. God has always intended to give us Love. Love comes from God. We are unable to produce it. God has given each of us power, Love, and peace. We should believe that we can forget and move on.

We must learn by growing, improvising, adapting, and changing ourselves, not others.

I have met some people who will be alone for the rest of their lives unless they can fix or remove their memories of the past. If this is you, I respect your choice. However, I hope that this book will unlock the prison door that has held you for so long. This door exists only in your heart or mind.

Notice I didn't say "doors" but "door." There is only one door that needs to open for you to walk out from fear into Love. But if you refuse to let go, then find comfort in your self-made prison cell and leave others alone.

This fear can only be managed by gaining the skills, tools, and abilities that give you discipline and insight into relationship-building. Notice that in the AMPC version, it says, "Personal discipline [abilities that result in a calm, well-balanced mind and self-control.]"

I know this place does exist. It is available to all who will go, grow, and become more loving by practicing loving in each opportunity that the Lord brings into their journey of singleness. Each day, I rise with the power to Love and the peace of knowing that I am well equipped to handle whatever happens. I am very thankful for the Word of God, inspired by the Spirit, which tells us that God has not given us the spirit of fear. All we have to do is accept that fear is not from God. Therefore, I will not receive it. God is Love.

Why not make this affirmation? "I can love. I will love. I shall find

Love in my life and have the Love of my life." Declare this and feel the power and peace of mind and heart.

Ask of the Father, and He will guide you to a place where fear is powerless and Love is ever-growing within our hearts and souls.

Love Lessons from Chapter 7

While the Spirit of the Lord has opened your mind and soul, remember the times when you may have been hedged into a place where you knew you should not have been. Did you see the light of guidance during that time? This is a good time to ask for help from the Spirit of Grace in your desire to discover the Love of your life by His guidance. Use the page of reflections for chapter 7 and write these moments down. What did the light reveal to you?

REFLECTIONS FOR CHAPTER 7

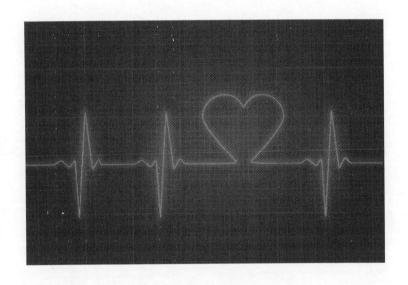

Perfect Love casts out fear.

—1 John 4:18

CHAPTER 8
Now Is the Time

Why remain in fear of Love when Love is available to remove all fear? My prayer is that you have found this book a source of enlightenment in your journey of singleness or pursuit of Love. Now is the time to realize that you don't have forever to allow Love to be present in your life.

The Bible says that faith is the substance of things hoped for and the evidence of things unseen. Faith without works is dead. Faith comes by hearing, and hearing by the Word of God. One of the final and most important keys to faith is that faith works by Love. Now is the time to recognize that no one else will do this work for you.

I know some people will glance at this book and pass it by because they feel they are not afraid of Love or loving. This is exactly why fear will linger longer than it needs to. We have the power over all fear because we have been given the Love that is needed to conquer all fear. This book is for you and for your entire Love life, not for your friend or associate whose pain you have helped to console. Now is the time for you to grow and go beyond where you have been by becoming what you seek in another.

Now Is the Time

Faith moves you to get beyond where you have been. Learn to use the fuel of fear to ignite the faith that will challenge you to go, grow, and get beyond the obstacles in your path of joy, peace, and Love. I am going to say this by faith: because you chose to read this book, good things will begin to happen in your Love life that you have never witnessed before. The reason that I believe this is that when you get the log out of your eye, you will notice the small speck in others' eyes. You will begin to reward yourself by saying, "Wow, I have grown and gone beyond where they are." However, you know that only God knows how you got there: from faith working by Love. You were obedient and willing to make some necessary changes in your approach. Instead of freezing up, rejecting, and resisting, you can now rejoice and receive and be rewarded by letting go of fear and using it to guide you into becoming a more loving person. You will discover that this is just a journey. The outcome will be good because of the experiences that lead you upward, not backward. Without fear, there can be no true appreciation for the Love that is produced. So your faith can turn the table on fear, making it your servant and not a continual tormentor.

Love is from God. God has put Love into your life—not just for you, but for another. You may be the turning point in another's Love walk, enabling both of you to be winners. There are no losers when we are freed from the fear that has kept us from giving what neither of us has had before. Love has to be sown and cultivated. It wasn't there before, but it's here now. Why question it? Why not give it? It doesn't belong to you. It's just passing through you on its way to where God intends for it to be.

Now is the time. Again, I am no expert. I am still single and learning. God is truly at work in each of our lives, to will and to do for His good pleasure. And we know that God causes all things to work together for good to those who love God, to those who are called according to His purpose (see Rom. 8:28). Again, I reiterate: *God is Love.*

> Who will separate us from the love of Christ? tribulation, or distress, or persecution, or famine, or nakedness, or peril, or sword?
> Just as it is written, "FOR YOUR SAKE WE ARE BEING PUT TO DEATH ALL DAY WE WERE CONSIDERED AS SHEEP TO BE SLAUGHTERED."
> But in all these things we overwhelmingly conquer through Him who loved us.

> For I am convinced that neither death, nor life, nor angels, now principalities, nor things present, nor things to come, nor power,
> nor height, nor depth, nor any other created thing, will be able to separate us from the love of God, which is in Christ Jesus our Lord. (Rom. 8:35–39)

I put this here because some have never had Love mature in their lives. But once we are able to push past fear, we will gain a Love that brings us together and makes us inseparable.

Now is the time for you to grow to this place in your life of wanting more than the same results, of starting and stopping, of blaming and remaining in heartache. So, with a loud voice, say yes! Say yes to Love! Say yes to loving again!

Yes is a powerful affirmation. It releases power within us. It enables each of us to do something instead of just whine and complain. We've all got war stories and memories of our failures and past pain from broken relationships. Now is the time to move forth and say no more. Now is the time to let go and let God lead you to still waters and green pastures. By using the journey of singleness, He will restore our souls.

On New Year's Day 2004, when I prayed, something happened. I believe that my heavenly Father began the process of restoring my soul. That is the way some of our prayers will be answered—not by giving us what we are requesting, but by preparing us for that gift when the time comes. For that I can now say, "Yes, yes, *yes!*" What a word from the Spirit of God. What a time for it to be released. "Move forth and say no more!"

The time is now. Something has begun to stir within your soul to let you know that it is time to move beyond the sitting, the mental tread milling, and the fear of being hurt. Yes will lead each of us to new opportunities and new doors opening. Then divine healing will be released like the morning dew. At times it may just be enough for a moment, a day, or a week. However, the process will keep you moving forward and not backward.

There are times when I look back and it all seems like a fog. It becomes really hard to remember past pain when the light of heaven has shone within one's soul. He is our good Shepherd. Yes indeed, He is. He only knows one way to lead us, and that is toward restoration of all things.

Scripture speaks of God making all things new. Remember, each time you allow yourself to push past the fear that arises when Love is really speaking, you will see the bright side someday.

Now is the time to act and accept the journey of singleness. It is God's path of corrections needed to lead us to His righteousness, for His name's sake, when it comes to growing and going beyond fear. God is at work within us, to will and to do for His good pleasure. He knows that we are in no way ready for His best, but we are still candidates for His best.

This is what has steadied my course through the years. I know there is a bright side somewhere. Someday, it will break through, because I pushed through momentary afflictions to behold an eternal weight of glory. When you do look back, instead of thoughts of hurt and pain, you may see the thorns, logs, and splinters that were in your heart and have been removed. Your heart and soul have been healed and restored. That, my friend, is nothing less than a miracle.

We are all works in progress and must remember that moving forward takes daily practice, practice, and more practice. There will be times when it seems like you are stuck and right back at the starting line. Just know that His staff is guiding you. The good Shepherd was at that place long before you ever got there. He knows you will not be camping there. You will be moving on and will see that moment as a time of teaching, letting you learn of the progress that your soul has made.

No matter whom you meet or where others may be, know that He is with you. It's your journey. The time is now to feel the fear but keep going and growing. You are becoming more loving and more able to be loved and give Love to whomever it is put in your heart for.

Remember, Love doesn't seek its own, nor does it keep record of wrongs suffered. Love comes from God. When it is harvested, it will remain, no matter what comes across its path. Nothing will be able to pull you apart from the one you love—absolutely nothing.

The only thing to fear is never experiencing "this kind of Love." This kind of Love will cast out all fear. Now is the time. So start the process for Love to begin in your life by not being afraid to love another. I pray this poem will become your reality of Love.

THE LOVE IN YOU

That Love that I know
Is much greater than
The Love I once
Thought I knew
This Love is full of life
It will continue to grow
Being nurtured by time
As we continue to sow
The Love in you
Is so flowing
It sweeps and dashes
Deep inside my soul
This Love I always looked for
This Love was hard to find
This Love comes from giving it all
No matter the day or time
I never knew it
Before it appeared
But I was aware
Of its existence
It was you
Who possessed such Love
The Love in you
That comes only from above
That gave to me the Love
To give to you

Priceless Production

Love overcomes all fears

Love Lessons from Chapter 8

May you reflect upon how you know that now is the time for you to begin to deal with your fears of loving? Bring those fears to the Lord, and allow His Spirit to speak to your heart concerning your singleness journey. Write down the things that you know you can practice to keep moving forward, becoming more loving and lovable. Speak these daily affirmations, especially when fear raises it head.

I am loving, I am lovable, and I can love again.

I can love, I will love, I shall find Love in my life, and I shall have the Love of my life.

REFLECTIONS FOR CHAPTER 8

Love never fails

—Apostle Paul

CONCLUSION

Even as I complete this work, I believe there is much I have left out that could be of benefit to another soul in their search for lasting Love. Today in my journey of singleness, I am seeing a change in the landscape that makes me give glory to God for listening to Him. I would have been married several times by now if I hadn't heeded that voice on New Year's Day 2004. I am seeing many people who have already entered into their third and fourth marriages at barely fifty years old.

I believe that this book will be a great tool to allow one to search inward and upward for the power of Love that can heal the brokenhearted. I know that His anointing will embrace those who make this a serious read for discovering the Love of their lives. No matter where you may find yourself on your singleness journey, I hope this book has assisted you to realize the destructive and tormenting power of fear. I hope it has opened the eyes of your understanding to the need to push beyond pain and fear, directed by the power of Love. Fear is real in all our lives. We never get rid of it. But we learn to manage it and embrace it, knowing that nothing can stop our pursuit of Love.

My prayer is that this book does for you what the Spirit of the Lord have done for me in making me realize that I needed help. It feels good to be able to see from within why we have made some of our choices in life. It is much better when we can eliminate those few specks, so we can truly see where we are heading. We will attract where we are.

My hope is that you find this work practical and beneficial in looking inward and upward, seeing the great Love that God has bestowed upon us all. Nothing is or has ever been wrong with Love. In the Beatitudes, Christ mentioned that the pure in heart shall see God. I believe that this book will enable you to begin to allow the purifying fires of the Holy

Spirit to burn out the lingering splinters of fear, allowing our hearts to see Love in a whole new dimension.

God is Love, and *Love never fails*. So take the spiritual notes that He has given you about your Love life, and allow the Spirit of Love to fill your life with new expectations. You may want to take the season of your singleness to practice and actively use the skills, tools, and abilities that remove fear and allow Love to do its work within you.

I hope that this simple book will release in you the need to seek God for more assistance. I believe there are many resources available when we find the need for them. He will guide you to these resources that you may have never even desired to look into before now.

Please join me in a prayer for your journey of singleness. I hope for the beginning of a new life leading to Love and the removal of all fear.

Our heavenly Father,

Thank You for allowing Your Spirit to draw those who have read this book. Help them begin to grow in grace and knowledge of You, a loving God. I ask that they are willing to be honest and accept change, for their best days are yet to come. I ask that they will allow Love to guide them from all their fear and past setbacks. I ask that they will be aware of Your presence guiding them to see the errors of their ways, and that they will know that You have brought them to this day of awareness—a new day in the life of singleness, a time of opportunity to prepare and make ready, a time to discover what You have prepared for them. I ask, Lord, that when that day should come, they will be reminded that it wasn't by their works but by Your grace, mercy, and works of Love. Therefore, I ask that they will give their best Love to the Love that comes from above, a true, healthy, and lasting Love that only You could have provided for them. I ask that the eyes of their understanding concerning singleness and Love will be opened, and that they may see as never before the gateway to Love.

In Jesus's name,

I offer this prayer,

Amen.

Pastor Tony K. Thomas

I hope that during the reading of this work, you will experience His divine presence within your heart and soul. I felt His presence so many times that I had to stop writing and just wait until I knew that I could do it. This work took me more than six years to prepare for and seven years to complete. Therefore, I believe that this isn't a work that you can read quickly. You must allow these thoughts of the heart to percolate and reveal your personal journey of singleness. The Holy Spirit will bring back to your remembrance situations that you now know you could handle better. This book is for your betterment; it is meant for you to begin to see that the Helper is at work. I hope that you will see the benefits of this writing and know that it is God-sent. We all have shared and listened to the war stories of broken relationships from others we know—friends, family, church members, coworkers, and even new acquaintances. Perhaps you will purchase a copy of this book for them or share it with them.

This book is just an eye-opener that will get you started and keep you on the path of His promises for you. I believe that if our eyes are clear, then we can see; if our ears are clear, then we can hear what the Spirit has to say concerning our hearts' desires. Our Father wants to give each of us His best. Know this: a better you will make everything much better.

If you are interested in further information about books, CDs, DVDs, or available teachings by Apostle Tony K. Thomas, you may e-mail fopoms@aol.com or write to:

    Foundation of Power Outreach Ministries
    PO Box 4913
    Sanford, NC 27331

    Or visit the following website for books by Rev. Tony K. Thomas:

    www.revtonykthomasbooks.com

THE LOVE WE HAD

Now that we must go our separate ways
We may never be together another day
But the fun we had will become memories
The Love we shared will drift off to sea

Soon we will move on
From all that once was ours
The giving, the sharing
Now becomes dust in our tomorrows

What took away such sweet moments?
It must have been more powerful
Than the greatest power
Mankind has known, Love

Strangely we never prepared for such
Instead we were just into one another
Never noticing
An enemy nearly approaching

The Love we had
It was just as real
As any Love given
For two people to cherish

Well, now that it's been replaced
By this distance between us today
Will we learn from our mistakes?
Or just wish each other the best?

We should have protected
The Love that we had
Should have made it first
Not just something else

Then we would have gotten beyond
This same place we have been
With others who came before
The Love we had

Love never fails
It has its own security system
It alerts each with alarms
To say, "Get working on it"

The Love we had
Could have enabled us
To work through each attack
Because it wasn't greater
Than the Love we had

Priceless Production

The Lord has called me to proclaim His glory to those who can't see and happiness to those who only know grief, pain, and misery. For all shall be made new through His mercies and riches in glory.

—Rev. Tony K. Thomas
August 8, 1982

ACKNOWLEDGMENTS

I am very humble and submitted to the call of Christ in my life. To the Godhead, I say, as I have said so many times, "Use me."

I give all honors to Him who called me in 1982. He is alive and lives forevermore.

Words cannot express my thanks to those who supported me with their prayers and thoughts of encouragement. I'd like to thank the body of Christ that I pastor at Foundation of Power Outreach Ministries in Sanford, North Carolina. I thank you for being there and allowing me to pour out of my soul all that the Holy Spirit has breathed and poured into it. I know it isn't easy to believe in the unseen and to learn about the unknown. Yet we have witnessed some powerful visitation and the very presence of our Father, His Son, and the blessed Holy Spirit at times in the small but mighty setting of our church.

Very special thanks to the faithful few who attend Sunday school and midweek Bible study. This is where we really connect and develop as believers in Christ.

Also, I'd like to thank those who have crossed my path in this journey of singleness after divorce. None of you knew, as I didn't know, that the time was for training in an area that is so much needed in our society. The area is how to navigate singleness. Whether Christian or not, we all need to gain tools, skills, and abilities to make this journey a fulfillment of our prayers and His promise. Many of those who walked with me for a short period did, after our time together, enter into that promise of marriage. I often wonder if I had a part to play in their promises being fulfilled. *I believe that we all contribute to others' success if our goal is for anothers' best.* God uses others to be instruments of His helping and healing hands in our lives.

I want to give a shout of appreciation for all the pastors, evangelists, teachers, apostles, and prophets from whom I learned and to whom I listened during thirty-six years of salvation. Many have gone on to be with the Lord, but their works continue as their pupil continues to share from the fruit of their ministries. I do not mention names, for they all have received new names that no man knows except our Lord Jesus.

Last but not least, I want to acknowledge you, the reader of this book. If it spoke to your life, then I know my purpose for sharing is worth it all. I believe, as my Lord said, in "what will a person give in exchange for their soul." One lost sheep shown the way back is worth more than the ninety-nine that already know the way.

I look forward to hearing about your successes along this journey of singleness, and the rewards of discovering that perfect Love casts out all fear. Again, remember these words of Christ our Savior: "Only the pure in heart shall see God." Remove fear, and you will see Love as never before.

Apostle Tony K. Thomas
Bond Servant of Our Lord and Savior

If you are interested in further information about books, CDs, DVDs, or available teachings by Pastor Thomas, you may email fopoms@aol.com or write to:

Foundation of Power Outreach Ministries
PO Box 4913
Sanford, NC 27331

Or visit the following website for books by Rev. Tony K. Thomas:

www.revtonykthomasbooks.com

A man's gift makes room for Him
And brings him before great men.

—Proverbs 18:16

ABOUT REV. TONY K. THOMAS

Rev. Thomas grew up in a very humble rural community in central North Carolina. Moncure was a community of 400 people, 399 when he wasn't there. Moncure has no stoplight, no major grocery chain, no internet, no cable TV, and no bank. It is a manufacturing and farming community divided by railroad tracks that formerly separated people along a racial divide.

Rev. Thomas grew up in a two-story home that was once the community's African American schoolhouse, before World War II. He shared that space with his father, mother, and six siblings. He was number six of seven. Growing up, he would find himself staring into some of the books still in the home. Even before he could read and write, he took an interest in learning. He always asked questions: why, what, when, and how.

Many of his initial Sunday school teachers were fascinated at his questions and his expression of dreams and visions that he had as a very young child. He was often told that he would be a preacher. Like many young people, Rev. Thomas wanted to be anything but a preacher. He saw being a pastor as being like an adult day care supervisor—someone who just refereed community conflicts. Therefore, he set his sights on science.

The Apollo space program had a great effect upon his life. He wanted to shoot for the stars and become an astronaut. That goal landed him many opportunities with major universities across the USA, studying in the fields of engineering and science.

After much thought, Rev. Thomas chose North Carolina State University for his undergraduate studies, first in civil engineering and later in material engineering and science. He discovered that college classwork and expectations were much more difficult than high school.

He had to learn to set goals and focus to be successful in obtaining a college degree.

Because of much misuse of time, he found himself flunking out of college. One day, he was told to just quit and not spend any more time or money in pursuit of his dream. He left that meeting dejected. He returned to his dorm room to ponder his next move. He decided that he would leave town unannounced and travel to California. He planned to get as far away from college as possible, get high, and let life find him.

To his surprise, something inside him spoke to him, It told him to go see his former materials engineering advisor to discuss his situation. Dr. Leon Jordan was leaving the university to pursue a musical career with a big band. He spoke to Rev. Thomas about being a diamond in the rough. He said, "You can graduate, but you are going to have to buckle down." That brought a new light into Rev. Thomas's soul. He went to celebrate with his college mates, whom he had left waiting in his room, doing his drugs, on that cold, snowy day in January 1982.

He was surprised to find no one there. But he wasn't alone. Like a voice out of heaven, from within his heart he heard the words, "You have been a fool." The scales immediately fell from his eyes. He saw his life pass in a flash. He knew that he had been foolishly living his life for fun and pleasure. The voice from within his heart sounded like thunder that shook his soul from the inside.

Rev. Thomas confessed his sins and admitted that he had been a fool. This was big. He had believed that he was intelligent, and that religion was for weak people who were losers in life. Once he said the words of confession and acknowledgment of his sins, he felt like a giant burden had been lifted from his shoulders. He was moved to open his Bible.

At the time, Rev. Thomas only had a Gideon New Testament Bible that he had received in third or fourth grade. The small burgundy Bible fell open to the gospel of Luke:

> And why call ye me, LORD, LORD, and do not the things which I say?
> Whosoever cometh to me, and heareth my sayings, and doeth them, I will shew you to whom he is like:

> He is like a man which built an house, and digged deep, and laid the foundation on a rock: and when the flood arose, the stream beat vehemently upon that house, and could not shake it: for it was founded upon a rock.
>
> But he that heareth, and doeth not, is like a man that without a foundation built an house upon the earth; against which the stream did beat vehemently, and immediately it fell; and the ruin of that house was great. (Luke 6:46–49 KJV)

The words screamed at him like thunder. The ruin of that house was great! This was a true God moment. Rev. Thomas acknowledged his sins before a living and holy God.

This was the beginning of a new life and walk with the Lord. It was revealed that Rev. Thomas would not just graduate, but would graduate by walking in the Spirit. Rev. Thomas completed his undergraduate degree and spent his final two semesters on the dean's list, something he had never accomplished before.

On August 8, 1982, Rev. Thomas, at the age of twenty-two, accepted the call of Christ in his life to proclaim the gospel. He preached his initial sermon in October that same year and was licensed as a local preacher. He began to teach Sunday school and Bible study, with occasional speaking engagements whenever the doors were opened.

In December 1983, he married. In 1984 he was ordained by Free Spirit Bible Church in Moncure, North Carolina, and later that year he enrolled in New Life Bible College in Cleveland, Tennessee, where Dr. Novel Hayes was the founder. He graduated from NLBC with honors in 1985, and was selected the class president during his attendance. In 1986, he was ordained and received a certificate of ministry from the Bread from Heaven Institute in Creedmoor, North Carolina, under the leadership of the late Dr. Mack Timberlake and Elder Brenda Timberlake.

Soon after praying for direction from the Spirit of the Lord, Rev. Thomas was impressed to unlearn all that he had studied before and come unto the Spirit and be taught. He became a student of the Word. He began to do as David mentioned in Psalm 1: meditate day and night upon the Word of God.

Rev. Thomas attended various ministries and serves as a teacher, evangelist, and prophet. He believed in the power of intercession and prayer, and often was a voice of guidance for the ministries. He remained in such capacity until August 1994, when he was commissioned by the Lord to return home to reach his family and start Foundation of Power Outreach Ministries in Sanford, North Carolina. He has been faithful to that call and continues in it to this very day.

Rev. Thomas is the father of two lovely daughters, Janelle and Tiffany, from his marriage. However, in 2003, he found himself in a new arena of life that he had never envisioned. He became divorced. He continued to be faithful to the call on his life by pouring out what the Spirit had poured in.

Rev. Thomas was instructed in his early years of ministry not to seek to write a book. However, in 2005, he was told to prepare to publish the messages that the Lord has given to him. He remembered the initial word from the Lord and did not seek to publish. He did continue to seek the Lord for further word concerning publication. After much wrestling and waiting, he began to open up his spirit to thoughts of writing for the Lord.

In 2011, after a few failed attempts at moving beyond singleness into a loving and lasting relationship, Rev. Thomas was given the assignment to write about the journey of singleness, in order to assist others in receiving the promise from God of oneness. He began to write one book in October 2011. In February 2012, he was instructed to begin work on another book. Through much prayer and discussions with the Spirit of God, Rev. Thomas has completed these works almost simultaneously.

The Lord instructed him many times that He would guide Rev. Thomas in writing the books. Rev. Thomas became a willing vessel to be used by God again in another aspect of ministry. After more than six years of struggling to complete the work, he finally realized that God was more than capable of writing a book through him. God wrote the most important books ever given to man—the books that make up the Bible. God uses men and women chosen to be instruments for His glory. Therefore, the endorsement of this book has been the prayers, the fasting, the patience, and the obedience of allowing the Spirit to breathe in these words and chapters in a time of need.

During these years and decades, Rev. Thomas also worked as a civil engineer and professional licensed surveyor for state and local government agencies in North Carolina. In September 2016, Rev. Thomas entered another new dimension by retiring from public work. Now he can finally focus on his true Love: the Word of God and the building up of the body of Christ.

After thirty-six years of ministry and more than twenty-five years of pastoring, Rev. Thomas still feels that he has not accomplished much for the Lord. He is still inspired and hungry to be used by God for His kingdom mission, to win the lost and keep the found. These books are subjects that come from the weakest areas in Rev. Thomas's life; however, they have made him seek God more to bring forth these works for the body of Christ.

To God be the glory, for He chooses the foolish to confound the wise. Rev. Thomas is still a fool for Jesus, with a fresh anointing for souls in all walks, races, nationalities, and statuses in life. His hope is that each person will be called to align their hearts and souls with the One who is above all things—Jesus Christ, Lord and Savior for the entire world.

Printed in the United States
By Bookmasters